"The Truth About yearning, of guilt, of unfulfilled wishes, of regrets, past and present, but more than these things, it is a quiet prayer for peace in a tumultuous relationship between a daughter and her father. The main characters are complex, contradictory, and vulnerable in their alone-ness and connections to themselves and each other. Lillibridge has woven a deeply moving assemblage of memories, each shining light into the quagmire of family."

–**Kao Kalia Yang**, author of *The Song Poet: a Memoir of my Father*

The Truth About Unringing Phones is heartbreakingly beautiful. Full of both darkness and light, Lara Lillibridge honors both the full weight of her love for her father and the complicated, and often painful, foundation on which that love, and all the memories surrounding it, was built.

–**Athena Dixon**, author of *The Loneliness Files*

"What a beautiful thing to take the ugly messiness of family and make of it a search for solace. Much like the way memory works, these fragments and pieces and shells trace the history and frustration of an estranged father-daughter relationship. They tell a story of longing, and loss. Of where love goes when it gets lost itself. They tell a story as old as time, or the day the first daughter was born and the first father came into being."

–**Paul Creshaw**, author of *Melt with Me: Coming of Age and Other '80s Perils* and Pushcart Prize Recipient 2017.

With admirable courage and raw candor, Lara Lillibridge chronicles the wrenching paradoxes that shaped her complicated relationship with her father in this stunning collection. The story's unconventional narrative structure that pairs long-form essay with searing, fragmented vignettes which mirror Lillibridge's journey to piece together the problematic dimensions of her absentee and neglectful father and to understand her place as daughter within that landscape. **The Truth About Unringing Phones** exemplifies how, amidst the heartbreak, threads of compassion, love, and grace can still be woven into the fabric of our most difficult relationships.

—**Melanie Brooks**, author of *A Hard Silence* and *Writing Hard Stories*

THE TRUTH ABOUT UNRINGING PHONES
ESSAYS ON YEARNING

LARA LILLIBRIDGE

THE TRUTH ABOUT UNRINGING PHONES: ESSAYS ON YEARNING
Copyright © 2024 Lara Lillibridge
All Rights Reserved.
Published by Unsolicited Press.
Printed in the United States of America.
First Edition.

No part of this book may be used or reproduced in any manner whatsoever without written permission except in the case of brief quotations embodied in critical articles or reviews.

Attention schools and businesses: for discounted copies on large orders, please contact the publisher directly.

For information contact:
Unsolicited Press
Portland, Oregon
www.unsolicitedpress.com
orders@unsolicitedpress.com
619-354-8005

Front Cover Design: Kathryn Gerhardt
Editor: Sara Casten; S.R. Stewart

ISBN: 978-1-956692-77-8

A Justifiable Unjustified Fear of Spiders was first published in *Thirteen Ways Magazine*, now defunct.

Essay Notes on Attachment Disorder was first published in American Literary Review as the 2016 Creative Nonfiction Contest winner, judged by Charles D'Ambrosio.

Memory Dissection: A Statue, My Father, and a Camera was first published in ROAR, now defunct.

The Right Tap was first published in *Hippocampus Magazine*, 2016.

Table of Contents

Introduction	13
The Many Wives of Clinton Lillibridge	15
Essay Notes on Attachment Disorder	16
From the Alaska Statutes	35
The Truth About Unringing Phones	36
Laranme and Juli	40
My Sister's Son, 2018	49
Unavailable, Unobtainable, Inappropriate (I love you)	48
Confession: An Exploration of Guilt and Secrets	58
I remember, I wonder, I want	64
Fragment of Yearning: Choices	70
Dementia, 2018-2019	72
An Illustrative Example	77
To Survive I Sold my Truth.	80
Liminal Space of 30,000 Feet	82
Bing. Are we there yet?	84
It's Not as if My Father Did Nothing for Me	86
Escape from New York	88

The Right Tap	91
Moving My Stuff	97
Fragment of Yearning: Hope	102
Don't Give Baby Birds to Children to Raise	104
Underwear Regrets	111
Memory Dissection: A Statue, My Father, and a Camera	107
Fragments of Doubt	117
Second Chances	118
A Justifiable Unjustified Fear of Spiders	121
Multiple Choice	126
Where Are Daddy's Pants?	127
Floating on a River of Smoke	128
Fragments on Yearning: Texts	131
Scrapbook: Visit to Alaska February 12-28, 1982	132
Rejections	136
Wish Night	140
Labels Attached to my Father	142
Complicity	145
Bean Kitchen	150
Oh, Christmas Tree	152
Choosing Dad	157
Fragment of a Song	159

The Blue Hour	160
Field Notes on Damage	163
Disneyland Dad	168
Deleted Paragraph	170
Past Tenths	171
The Reno Air Races	174
On Forgetting	179
Gifts 2015	181
T-Mom	183
A Trip Which May or May Not Have Happened, Delayed by COVID	178
An Author Interview, During COVID Times	188
Fact Check: Anchorage Daily News	191
Fragment of Yearning: COVID Spring	202
Responsibility Versus Self-Preservation	203
Things I Have Sent My Father During COVID	205
Things I Don't Send My Father During COVID	207
Reunited	208
Instagram	209
Fragment on Yearning: Father's Day	210
The Boat Was Always the Best Part of my Father	211
Eclipse	215
An Email	217

Inherited Trauma and the Avoidance Thereof	218
Present Tense	220
Plinko: Fragments of Resolution, or The Next Stage of Grieving	219
Finality	222
Closure	223
The Ending	231

THE TRUTH ABOUT UNRINGING PHONES
ESSAYS ON YEARNING

LARA LILLIBRIDGE

Introduction

When I was four years old my father moved from Rochester, New York, to Anchorage, Alaska, a distance of over 4,000 miles. I spent my childhood chasing after him, flying a quarter of the way around the world to tug at the hem of his jacket, beg him to look at me.

As I aged, my adoration of my father and longing for him was layered over with anger, revulsion, and later pity like a hand-dipped candle, these new emotions fusing with, but not replacing the yearning, which remained at my core.

My father is in his eighties. Parkinson's has left him with an unstable gait. An old neck injury rendered his voice quiet and raspy. Dementia comes and goes and stays longer each time. My father is a lonely old man and society says I should be a dutiful daughter, but the only way I have survived my father was to cut myself off from him, having only the most superficial of interactions. This book is my attempt to weigh responsibility versus self-preservation.

The Many Wives of Clinton Lillibridge

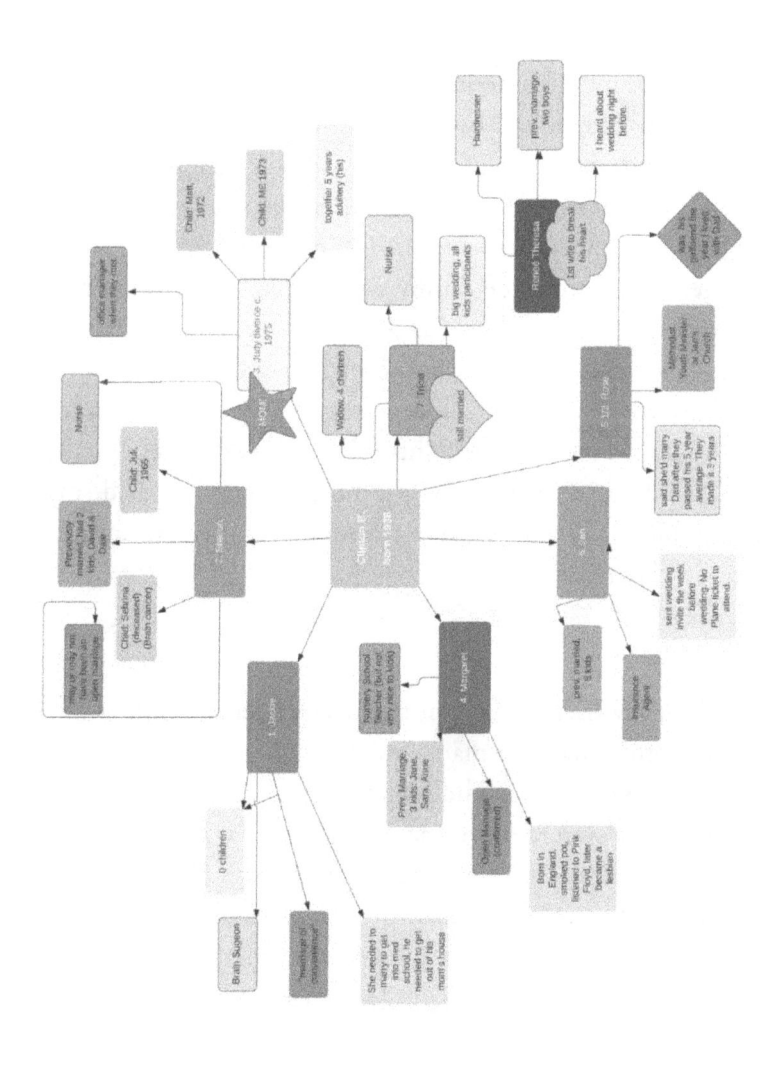

15

Essay Notes on Attachment Disorder

My Grandmother inherited one million dollars during the depression. She built a twenty-two-room house on ten acres of wooded beachfront property on Puget Sound in Washington state. The groundskeeper lived in a cabin at the edge of her land. There were maids' quarters with a separate kitchen and bath. The nanny only spoke to my father in French. My grandfather was a doctor, just like my father would become, and their house had an exam room with a separate entrance for when he needed to see someone in his off-hours. My father spent his whole life knowing that he would inherit a fortune. When my grandmother died, my father inherited only a silver tea service and a few antique wooden boats.

Consider:
> All of my friends thought that I was a liar when I said my father owned a plane and a boat, because both of my pairs of jeans had holes in the knees and my broken shoelaces were tied in knots. My father was a double specialist: pediatrics and gastroenterology. He did not save one penny of his earnings, and he cashed in my brother's and my trust fund to pay off his personal debts when we were in college. At age seventy-nine my

father lived in a small apartment and could only afford the gas money to go into town once a week.

When I was sixteen, I visited my father for a week in February and his cat ran away. My father's cat ran away and he put his arms around me and sobbed, shoulders heaving, snot unwiped from his face. He sobbed until my shirt was wet. It is the only time I remember watching my father cry. I wished at the time that I hadn't felt disgusted. When I was sixteen I visited my father and his cat ran away and he cried and I asked him why he hadn't become a veterinarian instead of a pediatrician. "I could never hurt an animal," he said. "I love animals too much to hurt them."

The red pebbly skin on my father's neck looks vulnerable and makes me feel somehow protective of him. I think I should knit him a scarf, but I do not know how to knit, and I could not sustain my affection long enough to complete the project. I do not know how to love or stop loving my father.

Define:
- *attachment:* a bond that transcends distance and time, a deep connection.
- *disorder:* untidy, messy, a state of confusion.
- *missing:* not present, gone, empty.

When I was ten, I was waiting for my father to finish his rounds at the hospital. When I was ten I was wearing a boys' shirt, light blue velour with a white placket and collar. It had been my brother's, and even though it was soft and even though my mother said that you couldn't tell it was a boy's shirt, I knew. I had big glasses, the plastic frames were golden brown on the outside edge, fading to clear by the nose. They were practical and identical to my mom's glasses. I wished they were red, and I wished that I was wearing a girl's shirt.

"Come see this baby," my father called to me. "It's the most beautiful baby I have ever seen."

I went into the hospital room and looked at the baby. It seemed nice.

I asked, thinking I was teasing, "Aren't you supposed to say I was the most beautiful baby you've ever seen?"

"You looked just like every other baby—kinda doughy. This baby, though, is really beautiful. Look how fine his (her?) features are."

On the ride home, I asked my father, "What color were my eyes when I was born?"

I knew the answer: my eyes were big and brown, and my mother told me that she saw my eyes in the delivery room mirror before I had fully emerged from her womb. She had told me over and over how my big brown eyes met hers when I was only halfway into this world. I had been told my whole life that my eyes were my best feature. I had my father's eyes, but my mother's coloring.

My dad answered, "The same grayish-blue as most newborns."

I suppose that I shouldn't be surprised that as his last child, my birth went hazy. As a pediatrician, he's seen hundreds of babies. He fathered four biological children, and step-parented another sixteen children through his seven marriages. Children are fungible, I should understand that. All kids need love; it would be petty to be jealous. I need to insert here that I am very petty when it comes to sharing my father with other people's children.

Revise to include:
How my heart exploded when my children were born. *Explode* as in *rupture, convulse,* or *burst.* How I still love to watch them when they sleep, though they are big and awkward and have bad breath sometimes and never comb their hair.

Fact:
The small sorrows experienced by my children wound me more deeply than the large sorrows of my own childhood memories.

Further clarify:
The love that I feel for my children makes my father's actions inexplicable to me.

My father called today, and I sent it to voicemail. Recorded words like *I love you,* like *you're so wonderful,* with added emphasis and devoid of feeling. I hit delete and didn't call him back. His strained voice infused guilt directly into my veins, but it was not enough to make me answer the next time he called.

My father had a sailboat and we sailed all summer. The deck was weathered gray teak. We scampered—little sea squirrels—in the cockpit and over the top of the cabin while the boat heeled steeply under sail. I held the tiller between my legs as I straddled the cockpit. I was too small to see over the windscreen otherwise. My father built us dinghies and we rowed races in deserted coves with seals and otters and puffins. We did not see people for days and our radio never worked. Once there was a storm and we had to sail all night, but I was not afraid because my father was invincible. I was a prepubescent ten-year-old with big teeth and unbrushed hair. We harvested mussels off the jagged rocks and ate them with butter. My father taught me to sew and bought me a wooden flute so that I could play songs to whales from the foredeck. My father played the autoharp and sang *Auralee* as the boat bobbed up and down, and he taught my brother and me to play, too, our voices and notes floating over the waves slapping the sides of the boat. He made us sit and listen while he read Jack London stories to us in the pale dusky evening of an Alaskan summer, even though we were too old to be read to anymore. There were porpoises and sea lions and bald eagles, killer whales—now called orcas—and big blue whales. The summer sun picked diamonds out of the jade green water and the raw blue topaz glaciers calved icebergs. My brother and I perched on the bowsprit as our father navigated the ice floe, responsible for spotting submerged icebergs lurking below the surface.

How do you sing a love song to a father you've hardened your heart against in order to survive him? Over and over years and years of wanting, hoping, ending in *silence*, ending in *no*, ending in *not enough*.

Consider:
- My father moved 4,171 miles away when I was three years old.
- From when I was four until I was sixteen, my brother and I spent a month or more of each summer, and two weeks every winter, in Alaska with our father. I spent both the visits and the time in-between visits in a constant state of yearning, as in unrequited, as in dejected.

When I was fourteen I lived with my father for five months. The night before Thanksgiving I went to my first sleepover since moving to Alaska. When I got home I discovered that my father had left for the church potluck without me. He had left me a note. *You are grounded off the phone for two weeks. You need to write a two-page paper on acceptable behavior for not coming home on time.* He had forgotten to tell me what time to be home, and at my mother's house, we never ate Thanksgiving dinner before noon. It hadn't occurred to me that he would leave the house at 10:00 a.m., or that he would leave me behind. He took the phone with him, so I couldn't call my mother or siblings or grandparents to say *Happy Thanksgiving*. I don't remember what I did besides writing him a few paragraphs on acceptable behavior, and a few pages on what I thought of him as a father. I must have eaten something, but it wasn't turkey.

When I was fourteen and lived with my father, he spent every night at his girlfriend's house. He came home every morning and made me peanut butter on toast for breakfast, sat on my bed, and watched me get dressed. When I was fourteen I did not want to be naked in front of my father but he was a doctor and I shouldn't be so sensitive; bodies were just bodies to him. He invited my nineteen-year-old boyfriend to spend a few nights with me while he was out of town. I did not know how to say in front of these two men that I hadn't decided if I liked this boyfriend enough to have sex with him. I was fourteen when my father gave me a twelve pack of condoms for Christmas and said, "Knowing you, these will be gone in a week." I have so many stories from these five months I lived with my father, but they all sound the same.

My father's eyes are large and cold blue, like the sky seen through an icicle. He seems to blink less than other human beings. He gives his full attention to whomever he is speaking with, but there is something cold and alien in his gaze.

Note for further speculation:
> He is a scientist and we are fascinating specimens. He is investigating, not relating. *Investigate* as in probe, inspect, and scrutinize. Feel the pressure swell into entrapment as the coverslip is set on the microscope

slide, watch the unblinking eye examine you minutely and ask you interesting questions.

Can an unblinking gaze be simultaneously friendly and sinister?

My father could do anything. He could build boats, sew open wounds shut, fly planes, wire a lamp, sail a boat on the open ocean. He could not love people, though he could say the words easily enough.

My father says:
- He was diagnosed with attachment disorder.
- He was the product of a rape of his mother by her husband.
- His mother wanted to drown him when he was born a boy.
- His father died of alcoholic cirrhosis of the liver. (My grandfather died of Parkinson's.)
- My mother left him for a woman. (My mother did not become a lesbian until several years after she divorced him for his infidelity.)
- My father says that it is not a lie if it makes the story better.
- My father is my only source for his diagnosis.

When I was nineteen, I got four new stepsiblings. The youngest were eight and ten, and the eldest were the same ages as my brother and me and out of the house already. They are the only stepchildren of whom I am not jealous. Their father died, so it was tolerable that they encroached on mine.

Of course that sentence is a lie—the one about jealousy—but it looks good on the page. My father taught them to ride bikes and went to their school concerts and took them to Hawaii, Mexico, and Europe. He bought them clothes and drove them to sleepovers and taught them to drive and bought them cars. He paid for one of their weddings and for another to attend boarding school in New Zealand. Of course, we all knew that Dad didn't want to do any of those things—he is only ever as good as the wife he married. The current wife, we'll call her Seven, made him send me postcards when he went out of town with her children. He had never sent me postcards before.

Consider:
- *diagnosis,* as in opinion, as in interpretation.
- *culpability,* as in blameworthiness, as in condemnation. Ponder whether it is nullified by the doctor's opinion, and if it matters whether the diagnostician is a medical doctor or merely a counselor. If one cannot feel empathy, can one feel remorse?

Answer the following:
Is it wrong to withhold love from a father who is incapable from birth of feeling empathy and forming attachments? What if he is old and lonely, and cannot

remember things clearly anymore? What if it is certain that giving in to this love will damage you again and again? The wretched yearning that you felt as a child still lives inside you, whether you hit ignore when he calls or not. The seal that you have made to contain it is not airtight.

A joke my father told me when I was ten years old:
"The Russian Ambassador and the African Ambassador were friends. One day the African Ambassador went to Russia to visit.

'This is our favorite game here; it's called Russian roulette,' the Russian Ambassador said. 'What you do is put one bullet in the chamber of the gun, spin the chamber, put the gun to your head and pull the trigger.' The African Ambassador thought this was a very good game and they played it several times. The next month, the Russian Ambassador went to Africa to visit the African Ambassador.

'This is our version of African Roulette,' the African Ambassador said. 'Any of these six African women will give you a blow job,' he explained.

'But what's the risk?' the Russian ambassador asked. 'Where's the roulette?'

'One of them is a cannibal.'"

I had to ask what a blow job was. When he told me, I flushed scarlet and ran away.

Attachment disorder is marked by a lack of empathy. A competent doctor must hurt in order to heal, the hands remaining steady despite the screams caused by remedy. Once, I watched him stretch a twelve-year-old boy's esophagus, the boy crying and vomiting as my father methodically forced weighted rubber rods down his throat until they came back bloody. He wasn't cruel; it had to be done. "Don't worry," my dad explained, "I gave him an amnesiac drug. He won't remember any of this." I, however, could not forget. I have twisted and sobbed under his hands as his scalpel removed my splinters, begging him to stop, my older sister pleading for him to give me a break.

What if you rise above sympathy and there is no greater compassion, but only empty curiosity?

Observation:
> The sound you make when you try to erase a sentence with a worn-out pencil eraser, the metal cylinder scratching across the paper, and how that sound feels in your veins and your teeth.

Full text of the story garnered through phone calls with my cousin, sister, and eventually my father:

I have two half-sisters from my father's second marriage: Juli and Sebrina. I am from his third wife. Juli is eight years older than I am. Sebrina was two years older than Juli. Sebrina died of brain cancer before I was born.

My remaining sister has just one memory of Sebrina, the one who died. She remembers two girls sitting in a little red wagon. She reached back to hold her big sister's hand—small hands sticky-warm, heads together, giggling. After Sebrina died, my then-three-year-old living sister would escape into the streets at night, looking for her missing sibling.

Sebrina could not have anyone over to play. My sister scratched her face until it bled because the morphine made her nose itch. The neighborhood kids came over in hopes of watching her die.

My father said that Sebrina couldn't swallow very well with the cancer and the chemo and the morphine. She could only drink through a straw. Her pediatrician gave Dad a blank death certificate to fill in whenever he needed to. My father said that was technically illegal, but it was a professional courtesy given to doctors.

Sebrina slept in bed between her parents. Her mother took sleeping pills. Sebrina asked for a glass of milk in the middle of the night. Our father brought her milk but did not give her the required straw. He sat next to Sebrina in the middle of the night and watched her drown. He had tried everything he could, so he just let her go.

My sister's body was donated to the local medical school. My sister had been the youngest patient to receive chemotherapy in the state of Washington. My father said, "They would call us when they were done with this bit or that and ask if we wanted her back piecemeal. So we didn't bother to claim her body."

There was no body, so there was no grave. There was no grave, so there was no headstone. My father chose a photograph instead of an epitaph, oversized and matted in blue velvet. He said that he kept Sebrina's picture on his office wall so that parents of terminally ill children would trust him to understand. I think he meant this as a sign of compassion. I don't think he realized that it sounded like a business plan. My four-year-old sister had a charming smile and hair like that of a downy chick. As a child, I looked at the picture on the wall and wished that I thought she was beautiful, but I couldn't get past her lack of hair.

My remaining sister baked cupcakes one year on Sebrina's birthday. She gave me a photo of Sebrina before she had cancer, when she still had blond curls. I keep it in my china cabinet with other fragile things. I do not bake for ghosts but I type words on pages, words like *futile*, words like *unlamented grief*, words like *intangible sister*.

Simplify to the following:

My sister drowned drinking a glass of milk. My sister drowned drinking milk and my father looked on. My sister was going to die anyway. There was no law that allowed mercy killing. My father was a doctor. My father had a blank death certificate. My father had morphine. My sister drowned in a glass of milk and my father watched while his wife was sleeping.

When I was eight and my sister, Juli, was sixteen, our father left us alone in the woods for a week to manage his campground. There was no electricity, there was no running water, there was no telephone. There was no car in case of emergency, although there was a canoe my sister could row to a nearby hunting lodge. When I was eight and my sister was sixteen, two drunk campers came to our campsite and wouldn't leave. They were tall, bearded men, unwashed from living in the bush country. They thought that my sister was very pretty. When I was eight and my sister was sixteen, our father left us in the woods alone without a telephone and we had to lock ourselves in our cabin until the leering men went away. My sister told me, "If I tell you to run, go out the window as quietly as you can and climb in the window of the cabin next door. I'll meet you there. Don't look back or wait for me in the woods, just run as quietly as you can." My sister is fully grown now, and still only four-feet-nine-inches tall. I don't know how she was so brave that night. She says it was because she had already lost one sister, and she wasn't going to lose another one.

When I was thirty-four and divorced, my father bought tools for my new house. He built a railing in the attic to keep my children from falling over the edge. He gave me a yellow tape measure with a built-in laser level that he had borrowed from his wife's sister. He was supposed to return it, but he said that I needed it more. She had gotten divorced the previous month and was struggling with money and home repairs and all the same things that I was. He chose me over his sister-in-law and gave me her tape measure. I will resist the urge to meditate on the measure of a father. Some metaphors are too easy to have substance. I still have that tape measure. That was the same year he spent Christmas with his stepchildren in a scenic little cabin an hour from my sister's house. He didn't tell my sister that he was in town. His wife and replacement family don't like her very much.

A limerick, taught to me by my father when I was nine:
   Nymphomaniacal Jill
   tried dynamite for a thrill.
   They found her vagina in North Carolina
   and bits of her tits in Brazil.

When I was twenty, my father gave me away at my first wedding. My father insisted on wearing a different color bowtie and cummerbund than the rest of the wedding party. I begged him to pay the fifteen dollars to rent the matching tie, but he refused. My father insisted on wearing buttons in the shape of penguins down his white shirt. I begged him to take them off, but he refused. My father told me, "Slowly, slowly," as we started to walk down the aisle, and he looked at me with his big light blue unblinking somewhat psychotic eyes and I realized that I should have insisted that I take this walk with my mother and not my father. I looked at his reddened dry hand on my elbow and felt nothing at all. Don't worry—the marriage didn't last. I got married again and revised my choices the second time around.

My stepmother taped a photo of my shirtless father to my refrigerator door. His shaven, sagging chest repulsed me. I left the picture there until I moved away five years later.

I could neither stand to look at it, nor betray him by removing it.

- *betray,* as in forsake,
- *betray,* as in delude.
- Fact: I deluded my father by leaving it there, because I could not forsake him by throwing it away.

At the end of every childhood summer, my father threw a birthday party for me and invited every child we knew peripherally, because we had no real friends. We played limbo. There was a map and a treasure hunt. He bought me roller skates one year, but boys' blue skates instead of girls' white ones. At the end of every summer, we went home with a scrapbook my father made with captioned photographs and all of our drawings and every letter we had written to our mother that he had never mailed home.

Sketch for the reader:
> A six-year-old writing home with left-handed penmanship, yellow lined paper with cross-outs and erasures so determined they wore a hole through the paper. My mother checking the mailbox every day we were gone and coming away with empty hands.

When I was nearly forty my father came to visit and bought me a simple charcoal grill. He sat on the stairs of my front porch and looked at the diagram for the grill, then looked at the screw in his hand, then looked at the diagram, and then set down the screw. Then he picked up the screw and looked at the diagram again. I remembered watching him perform surgeries. I remembered watching him build boats. Plenty of times I had handed him tools while he fixed our diesel engine as we bobbed on the open sea. When I was nearly forty I watched my father pick up a screwdriver in one hand and a screw in the other and look at the diagram over and over as if it were a Dead Sea Scroll. His hands shook. My boyfriend sat down beside him and picked up the screwdriver because Paul could see that this man who used to save people's lives could no longer assemble a simple grill, and he didn't know how to say so. My father looked at Paul with chagrined gratitude. My father's knuckles were big and red, and the backs of his hands had ropy, thick blue veins. Later that day he asked me to make him a peanut butter sandwich. I realized that he had forgotten how.

There was something weird that happened in a bathtub with my father when I was small. I remember him asking, "Where's the penis?" I don't remember anything else. Perhaps the question was only an anatomy lesson. Perhaps I remember nothing else because nothing followed. I worry that if I try to remember too hard, I will fill in details with my imagination and no longer know what is true.

Furthermore:

- My father and his wife, Margaret, had sex while my brother and I were in the room. Afterwards, we snuggled in bed with them. We were all naked.
- My father walked around completely nude, and I could describe his blue-headed penis as easily as I could describe his bearded face.
- There was a bare-chested mermaid on his cribbage board, and a mug shaped like a breast where you drank out of the nipple.
- But my father never touched me.

Define:

- *covert* as in hidden, as in camouflaged, as in shame.
- *abuse* as in misdeed, as in perversion, as in wrong.
- *secret* as in ambiguous, as in furtive, as in all the things you did not tell your mother.

My father was the smartest man I knew. My father was a renowned physician in Alaska. My father was everyone's favorite dinner party guest because he was so attentively charming. My father lost privileges at Genesee Hospital after he had an affair with the mother of one of his special-needs patients, who then tried to commit suicide when my father tired of her. My father was a school nurse after he retired. My father wore a Dr. Seuss hat to school every day. My father was fired for looking at the students too closely, holding their hands too long.

THE TRUTH ABOUT UNRINGING PHONES

When I was three my brother and I spent every-other-weekend at our father's house, before he moved to Alaska. When I was three he locked us in the bedroom at night and left us an empty mayonnaise jar to pee in. When I was three I did not know how to squat over a jar to empty my bladder and urine ran down my legs as I pounded on the door and begged my father to let me go to the bathroom.

Revise to Include:

> You never feel anything when you see your father until the moment he walks away and it is too late to run after him crying, "Daddy, Daddy, come back." And in that moment you remember the feel of his scratchy wool coat under your cheek, and you remember when he twirled you around in circles and still your mouth remains closed as you turn away and drive back home.

From the Alaska Statutes

AS 25.20.030. Duty of Parent and Child to Maintain Each Other.

Each parent is bound to maintain the parent's children when poor and unable to work to maintain themselves. Each child is bound to maintain the child's parents in like circumstances.

Ten years ago, my father and his wife, Tricia, left Alaska to live closer to her four children in the Seattle-Tacoma area. My sister, Juli, lived nearby as well, though that didn't seem to be a factor in their decision, so evidenced by them not inviting her to holidays or family events.

By choosing to move to the lower 48, Dad has relieved his biological children of any legal obligation for his care.

If only morality was as easy to codify.

The Truth About Unringing Phones

My father didn't know I walked away from him. I just stopped answering the phone. Stopped scheduling visits. Stopped pretending. It took him years to notice I was gone.

Now he is the one who sits beside an unringing phone. He's no longer Daddy—just a father I used to know. Old. Broken down. His head filled with memories crumbling to shards. Flashes of images put back together with the wrong names attached.

I struggle not to call.

Calling only opens the wound that is scabbed, not yet scarred. I don't call and pretend I don't want to. He calls and I don't answer.

His time remaining is short. This is the last chance for what I never had. But I already know I never will get more than I have now. The only surprise is that I suddenly care again, years after walling off my heart. I blame Christmas, but that's not it. I only ever saw him on the holidays three times in my forty-seven years—not enough to justify nostalgia.

Somehow an image of him as he is now has gotten stuck inside my head. My disgust at his adult diapers, the scrape of kissing his sharp, scruffy cheek. The empty eyes of a man who was once the smartest person I knew. Perhaps this will be the winter of the final phone call, telling me he no longer waits by the phone for anyone.

How do you say goodbye to a father you've already abandoned?

Tucked in my closet is his old plaid coat, which I can neither bear to wear nor to throw away. It no longer smells of his warm neck but the scratch on my cheek is the same.

In an effort to shut off my yearning I focus on my white teddy bear. It was a Christmas gift from my Grandmother that last year of childhood, when I said I only wanted clothes but she somehow knew that deep down inside I needed a toy one last season. I remember the image of the empty bed and my father's voice as he told me he'd given the bear to his then wife's granddaughter. That was two wives ago and I wasn't invited to that wedding either, though she sent me a card the year after the divorce.

I try not to think about the way Dad's hands looked as they grasped the smooth brown tiller as he taught me to sail—his fingers red and the backs of his hands ropy with the same veins as on my own. The lilt in his voice as he taught me this one beloved thing. I haven't sailed in years. The last time I was on a boat I refused a turn at the helm. What was the point in it?

Instead I try to remember the postcards Dad sent when he took other people's children on vacation and I sat home alone. I want to recall the stuffy stillness of a house with an unringing phone. On my birthday. When I passed my road test. When my heart was broken or my dog died or the time I won the 100-yard dash. So many silences. But he always remembered the names of my friends though he'd never met them.

The problem is that the space I made when I walked away is filled with the echoes of his voice calling for me now that he is old and alone. The other children he chose over me don't want him either, not that they ever did. It was always their mother who forced them on each other.

And as for me, I was never enough for him to choose. No matter who was smarter, prettier, did better in school. Perhaps my inescapable failure birthed my apathy. I never was very good at having goals beyond having a family of my own. I gave up trying to win at anything back in ninth grade, and it wasn't until I became a mother that I allowed myself to dream again.

But Facebook posts show him smiling with other people's children, while my own sister wasn't invited to Thanksgiving, even though her son had died just three months before. I flew across the country for the funeral, and my father spent the morning at his step-granddaughter's third birthday and was late to the service. Life is for the living, he said. Weren't my sister and I still alive? He meant to be there earlier, but it was not his fault it started to rain.

I picture myself made of bronze. My cheek cold, my ears sealed shut. I wish and hope to be that taciturn and strong, but I am made of flesh and my heart still beats for him, though I tell myself over and over not to give in. And still I know I will mail gifts again this year and I will have to answer the phone on Christmas. And New Year's. And his birthday. And I know his faded voice will yearn for me, and still I will make excuses and hang up as soon as eight minutes are done.

Laranme and Juli

My brother and I were twins, except not really—we just liked to tell people we were because we wanted to be so badly. Matt was a head taller and eighteen months older than I was. He wore glasses from the age of three and I didn't until I was ten, but we had the same brown eyes, brown hair, side parts and cowlicks. We fought and rode bikes and raced to the corner store together. Granted, he was faster because he was bigger, but I was tougher and even if I couldn't hit as hard, I could outlast him. We watched TV side by side on the living room rug, shared books and sometimes traded socks when the dirty laundry piled up.

It was always Matt and I against the world.

I did not speak of "I" as a child. Everything was "we." Everything that happened to him, happened to me, at least vicariously. I cringed with every blow he took from our mom's partner, every insult hurled at him at school. In first grade, Matt spoke of Lara-and-me so often his teacher thought it was the name of an additional sibling: *Laranme*. We were separated by a single grade but we were one unit: the children.

I don't mean that we had everything in common. I loved dolls, he loved Transformers. I was a goody-goody; he didn't seem to mind being in trouble. In a lot of ways, we were very opposite, very different people. Yet, we saw the world through the same familial lens, we valued the same things, and while our scars weren't identical, they mimicked each other's. He was more like me than anyone else I knew.

If Matt was an extension of me, Juli was only half us. We all shared a father, but she was from wife #2, and we were from wife #3. Juli was eight years older than me, six years older than our brother. While Matt and I had brown eyes and nearly black hair, Juli had baby blue eyes and thick red locks. Matt and I were long and willowy, Juli was short and compact. Juli had a thyroid condition and never grew. Dad, a pediatrician, never noticed. Matt wound up six-feet-nine, Juli maxed out at four-feet-nine—technically a dwarf—and I was in the middle, at five-seven. We were stair steps, almost exactly a foot between each of us.

Matt and I devoured books and Juli had dyslexia. Matt and I were atheists and Juli sang Jesus songs and slowly and deliberately read the Bible to me at night, though we never got past Genesis. Matt and I were fearless when we sailed with Dad, and the one time Juli came with us she clutched me to her chest, crying in terror that we would crash.

Juli and I were summer sisters, and when autumn approached Matt and I went back to New York, and Juli flew home to Seattle.

Juli had a full sister once, long before I was born. Sebrina died of a brain tumor when she was seven and Juli was three.

Juli asked God to send her another sister, and when I was born she claimed me as her favorite. Juli curled my hair and looked out for me, but mostly ignored Matt, which was fine with him. Matt was used to being the eldest and he didn't like to be bossed around. Sometimes the two of them would argue, but I do not recall a single fight I had with my sister.

She always told me how we had a special bond. I never told her that it wasn't anything like the bond between me and my brother. She was my dream-sister, built on yearning, he was my confidant and co-conspirator, the person I walked to school with, ate bread-and-sugar with when there was nothing else sweet in the house. It was Matt I sat next to when we flew to Alaska. But I knew that I was all she had—a second chance for a sister.

Juli did have two older half-brothers on her mother's side—all grown up and out of the house—but no full sibling that belonged entirely to her. No *Juli-n-me*.

When she was sixteen, Juli had to take her mother off life support and after that, she had to move to Alaska for her last two years of high school. Once she graduated, when I was ten, she stopped coming up to Alaska for the whole summer, though she'd try to come up for a week when she could to see me—I knew it had nothing to do with missing Dad. I knew how he and our stepmother locked her in her room with granola bars and water for hours on end, how they made fun of her for never drinking nor smoking and being so good. Juli told me all her secrets as I sat in front of her on her bed and she brushed my hair.

I spent a week in Seattle with Juli the summer I turned twelve. She taught me how to shave my legs—I'd been using a razor and water, my lesbian parents not willing to encourage me in this endeavor. She showed me how to lather my legs first so the blade didn't sting. She cut my hair and we both slept in the queen-sized bed of her one-bedroom apartment.

Juli had gone to cosmetology school instead of college, so Dad agreed that he'd pay for her one-year program and then pay her rent for the first year after she graduated so that she could build a clientele. Since her child-support agreement required him to pay for her education and she wasn't going to a two- or four-year school, it was a good deal for both of them. The week before I visited her, which happened to be the last week of the month, Jan, Dad's wife #5, decided they weren't going to send the rent check the following week, or ever again. Her daughter—also nineteen—was pregnant and needed their financial support. Juli got a third job the next day, doing night inventory at a department store, and picked up more hours at Taco Bell in addition to the beauty salon. Juli didn't have time to waste on tears, she carried on doing what needed to be done to survive.

Dad's sister, Anne, took me to the grocery store, because Juli couldn't afford to feed an extra person for a week. Dad's mother wrote him out of her will and instead left the small caretaker's cabin to Juli so that she would always have a place to live. I didn't know these relatives that were so present in my sister's life and my father's past, and I was quiet around them, though they were kind to me. Juli was much more of a Lillibridge than I was by both proximity and appearance, her face a miniature feminine version of Dad's.

Juli and I took the bus and walked to the Golden Shears and Taco Bell, and I stayed home alone when I couldn't go to her job with her. But Juli never complained about walking or working. As we walked, she told me about her boyfriends, taught me church songs and football cheers, and when a friend of hers got us free tickets to the Seattle Center, it was like the universe or perhaps her God was taking care of us. I didn't have her faith but I could feel the warmth of it, the possibility.

Our sisterhood was shaped by a week together every year or two, buoyed up by letters and phone calls as I slowly grew up, and she married and became a mother. We talked on the phone as we planned our first and then second weddings, and we talked on the phone as we planned our first, and then second divorces. We talked about our lives as single mothers, discussed how to decorate on miniscule budgets, encouraged each other as we found jobs and tried to make ends meet. We cried on the phone over failed relationships and reassured each other by turn, alternating from consoled to consoler. It was always easier for me to see my sister's bad relationship decisions than my own. Even when I got frustrated with her, I always understood how being raised by our father shaped her choices, and I'm sure she would say the same for me. I am probably foolish when I think her decisions are worse than mine. Perhaps it is only worse luck.

As close as we were, I have seen her sons only a handful of times. When I gave birth to my first child, it had been nearly ten years since Juli and I had seen each other, but she flew across the country to hold her nephew in her hands.

I nursed my baby with one arm and hugged her with the other as she cried and confided that she was afraid her husband was cheating on her. She reorganized my house and gave my son a pacifier without my asking. I was frustrated and didn't know how to tell her to stop messing with my stuff or my parenting, but later I recognized the love and wisdom as my baby soothed himself to sleep.

After a few days we both agreed it was better for her to fly home a day early to surprise her husband and find out if he was cheating (he wasn't). She was loving and bossy and emotional, and I was thirty-two, leaking breastmilk and crying over sad TV commercials.

My fifteen-year-old son still has the mint green blanket she knitted him, and I take a picture of him with it every year on his birthday and text it to her. She's never met my youngest child, now twelve, but he knows who she is. They hear stories, even though they don't speak to her on the phone, nor do they exchange cards or gifts with her at birthdays or Christmas.

When our youngest stepsister, Kym, got married, she invited Juli and me, with the understanding that I would keep Juli out of her hair. "We love Juli, but you know..."

THE TRUTH ABOUT UNRINGING PHONES

I did know. Juli was divorced and sad and needy, but she was our sister, and she was so much more than her weakest moments. I knew I was all Juli needed to get through the wedding as an unwanted guest.

I flew across country for the wedding to Seattle, where all of my stepsiblings and Juli lived. At the airport, Juli launched herself at me as if we were still kids, hugging me hard. I felt less awkward than I feared I would—the angle of the air between us was familiar. I had forgotten how blue her eyes were until I saw them again. Her smile was the same. Her words—I'm not one who can recall someone's voice, I have no auditory memory, but when she spoke, my ears remembered the shape of her words, the pitch, the accent. You'd never mistake us for each other over the phone. Her inflections were west coast, mine east. Our slang was slightly different. And Juli still said "guy" instead of God, so she wouldn't swear and go to Hell. I said, "Jesus fucking Christ" and didn't feel bad about it. She gave up reprimanding me for it years ago.

We went shopping and bought matching shoes. Her rental house was filled with light and flowers. We slept again in her same queen-sized bed like we had twenty years before, only this time her long-haired chihuahua slept between us.

As we dressed for the wedding, we marveled over our aging adult bodies. Our feet and hands are the same, and we gain weight in the same places. Our wrinkle patterns are similar. She curled my hair, but I wouldn't let her do my makeup.

Our skin tones are too different, as is our idea of how much eyeshadow is enough.

We went to the wedding, which was beautiful, and Juli cried over being divorced and alone, but only a little bit.

After the wedding we helped clean up the guest house the bride had arranged for all her out of town guests—two big mansions with in-ground pools and ginormous kitchens overflowing with empty wine bottles and takeout cartons. All the bridesmaids had vanished for their return flights. Our stepmother, Tricia, was slowly trying to pack more things into her suitcases than was humanly possible. Juli and I did what we could, then left Dad and Tricia to sort the rest out on their own. I had my own flight to catch to return to my children and it wasn't my mess to clean.

Juli and I talked, as we always do, about visiting each other, but I always leave it as, "next year." We got along best with promises of somedays in a chain of daisies strung across the country between us. We are sisters built on dreams, and we don't have the scaffolding to support squabbles and arguments, which would inevitably happen if we lived in the same town. We have no history of screaming fits and making up again after.

Matt and I see each other every Christmas and for a week in the summer, sometimes a random day in-between if I'm going to be in town for a book event. Our kids love each other and play together even though there is a twelve-year span from my eldest to his youngest. Matt is still the person who best understands me without needing any backstory or explanation, and when we see each other, we speak in half-sentences, inside jokes and eyerolls, as if we were never apart.

But it is Juli I text every day. Even when the weight of her threatens to pull me under. I have not lost a child. I have not lost a mother, or my only full sibling. I knock wood as I write this, praying to continue to elude fate's hand, which hovered over the names of the two Lillibridge daughters and assigned these losses to my sister instead of me. Even when she is too much, too often, too needy and too broken-hearted. I am here to share the burden of her grief as much as I am able. That is what fate dealt me. And that is how I love my sister—inadequately and carried on the wisps of dreams instead of memories.

My Sister's Son, 2018

My sister handed me what looked like a fuzzy pillow. It was the container of her middle son's cremains, covered in a soft blanket.

"Hug him," she implored. "Hug Jacob."

It was surprisingly heavy, and the give of it was as if it was filled with sand. It gave, and then it didn't. I hugged it and I cried—of course I cried.

The service was delayed. Our father, his wife, and Kym were late. They were coming from a birthday party for Kym's three-year-old daughter—a party Juli and I were not invited to. I had raged at my father and his wife over their decision to attend the toddler party instead of supporting my sister, but it didn't change their minds.

Of our four stepsiblings, Kym was the only one who came to the funeral. After the service, Kym pulled me aside to confront me about how I portrayed her in an essay. She didn't mind that I wrote that she didn't like Juli very much. She minded that I said that our parents paid for her and her sibling's college tuition and weddings. She told me that she was self-made. I bit back my rebuttal and didn't argue. What can you say about an essay at a funeral for a boy who never reached thirty?

Our brother, Matt, did not come. He hadn't seen Jacob since our nephew was four. Matt and Juli aren't close. She didn't mind that he didn't come—he worked for a school district, it was the first week of classes, his wife had two toddlers at home. Juli didn't mind that our other stepsiblings didn't come, either. She didn't mind that we weren't invited to the party that morning. My sister has never learned to hold a grudge, while I gather mine to my chest and keep them close to me always. Juli would grieve her son with whomever was there to grieve alongside her.

The service was standing room only. Jacob had been a cook in a restaurant, and his co-workers served chicken and side dishes at the memorial, like the wedding he'd never have. We sat in chairs around tables with white tablecloths—those who could find seats. I stood against the wall, regretting the high heels that I wore to match my sister. She and I wore identical shirts with kittens on them that she picked out for us at Wal-Mart that morning. My sister loved matching clothes, sister mugs, anything that made us a set. Strangers could see that I belonged with her, even though we don't look anything alike. I liked not having to clarify who I was. The kittens explained it for me.

That morning I had sat with my oldest nephew, Jacob's brother Jonathon, and tried to help him write words to say at his brother's funeral. I was the writer, and he had no education beyond high school. I was supposed to be good at this. Inspiring. But I didn't know how to help someone find their words.

"Just write what you feel," I advised. "Whatever is running through your mind right at this moment. Just talk to him, or about him. Tell us your favorite stories."

"My mind is empty. I don't have words, I don't have memories right now," he told me. His long red beard was clean and shiny. I wondered if he brushed it. I remembered when Jon was five and wore a box over his head, and my first husband pushed him over for no reason. That wasn't a story fit for a eulogy. That was the trip, twenty-odd years ago, when we went to a lake, and I changed his youngest brother Daniel's diaper on a blanket in a field—Juli had to show me how to do it. The next day Jonathon and Jacob made a catapult to throw rocks, and Jacob wound up with stitches in his forehead.

The next time I saw Jacob, we were both adults, smoking cigarettes outside Juli's house. Jonathon had swung by for dinner one night. We were affectionate strangers, connected only through the waypoint of my sister.

In other words, I had no memories to give him.

I entered this loss as his mother's sister, not as his aunt, though I was of course both. But the twenty-six hundred miles between us meant Jacob was my sister's son more than he was my nephew.

THE TRUTH ABOUT UNRINGING PHONES

In the end, we decided Jonathon should read the Facebook post he'd written the day his brother died. It was the best we had, and I assured him that none of his friends would recognize that it was recycled material.

I met my sister's live-in boyfriend for the first time. He was pleasant, eager for my approval. We talked about dogs—a topic we could agree on. He had recently finished parole for something to do with teenage pornography that left him on the sexual predator registry and he had a brand-new confederate flag tattoo on his upper arm. Juli always sees the potential good in people, and always believes they can be redeemed. I'm not so certain.

The boyfriend left to buy dog food and was gone over three hours. I suspected another woman, but my sister pretended not to notice the length of his absence, so I didn't comment. At the funeral, the same boyfriend helped setup, clean up, and attended to every detail like a loving spouse should. He was unexpectedly perfect. I resisted liking him, but I was grateful that he took such good care of my sister that moment, when the loss of her son threatened to consume her.

When Dad and Tricia arrived, we found them chairs. I was glad it was too crowded to sit together, and simultaneously aggravated that their lateness made it so we could not do this one thing for my sister.

After the service my father pulled me aside and apologized for years of neglecting me and my biological siblings. I'd like to give you the dialog, but my anger acted as the flash bulb in an overexposed photograph, blurring details, leaving only his intention at the center, the rest out of focus. I avoided his direct gaze and looked instead at his *Grandpa-saurus Rex* T-shirt, which he hadn't changed out of after the birthday party.

My father's words didn't undo forty years of inaction, but I said something soothing. That is what you do at funerals.

Unavailable, Unobtainable, Inappropriate (I love you)

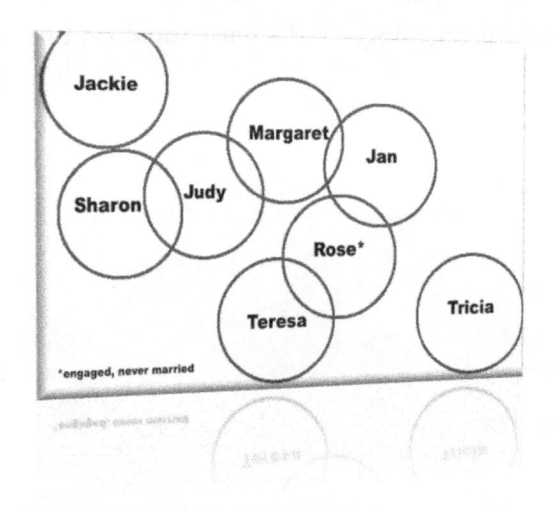

Diagram showing overlapping circles labeled: Jackie, Sharon, Judy, Margaret, Jan, Rose*, Teresa, Tricia. Note: "*engaged, never married"

My father was a hopeless romantic, and loved to fall in love, fall out of love, and then fall in love with someone else, get divorced, get remarried.

All his relationships overlapped, like beverage rings on an old desk, until Teresa. She kicked him out ten months after their marriage as soon as they bought a 6,000 square foot house "up the hill" in the rich part of town. She was, I think, the first woman to really break his heart. The rupture in his pattern—the ten months of being single after Teresa—is why Dad and Tricia are still together now, twenty years later.

Note: I do not technically know if all the wives were "other women." I know only that he secretly dated while married with all of them until Teresa, and some of them definitely overlapped, though they did not always know he was still married when they met him. I need to allow space for the women's potential innocence, though my father had none.

I didn't particularly like most of his wives and I wasn't particularly sad to see them go. Still, I thought about one or two of them (or their children) in unexpected moments, though I didn't dwell on it very much. All the family pictures and labels of stepsister or stepmother did not make any of my former family members remain in contact with me. When my dad broke up with them, they vanished from my life, and I from theirs.

But children watch their parents for clues to understand themselves as well as clues to how grownups act, even ones that live far away. I know I will love my kids forever, I know I will love my parents forever. I can't turn that love off. But I have not historically looked at marriage with the same eye. I will love you forever, unless you…until you…except if you….

I always worried I inherited some discontented gene from my father, making me incapable of life-long commitment. It was a matter of pride that I never cheated on anyone myself, but the threads of my brokenness mirrored my father's. I was a serial monogamist, but I didn't know how to mean "forever," though I was quick to say the words.

I spent years in relationships with unavailable people. It is only now that I see the unrequited longing for someone mimicked my bond with my father.

Unavailable People I've Dated:
- Man in California when I lived in Ohio
- Man in Chicago when I lived in Ohio
- Every person who kept me as a fallback in case they couldn't find someone better
- Man with girlfriend
- Married Man A
- Different Man with girlfriend
- Married Man B
- Married Woman

In all fairness to my father, my mother and her partner Pat had to give up everything for each other, too, being lesbians in the 1970s. Somehow my idea of love was a combination of both things: the yearning for what is not present and the idealization of the forbidden.

Other People I've Dated on the Socially Forbidden Side:
- Brennan, back in 8th grade, one of the few Black kids in school.

- I once had a crush on a skinhead in high school though I didn't know his name.
- That biker I married after first dating his younger brother.
- A Black woman from an island where no one spoke the word lesbian.
- A Palestinian Man (I'm half-Jewish on my mother's side).

I needed someone to give up everything for me, though I knew it wasn't right to ask.

I needed love to be what saved me. Transcendence. Disney Bluebirds forming a heart as we walked into the future leaving everything and everyone else behind.

Needy and selfish though I was, that married man eventually chose me, though a decade later I still carry the weight of our beginnings.

Confession: An Exploration of Guilt and Secrets

I have to tell you something ugly: when my father told me he was trans, my first response was rage. My guilt is deepened by the fact that he thought I was the safest to tell. Like during so many conversations with my father, I clutched the phone to my cheek and paced in circles in the backyard—the phone more tangible that he was.

I heard his confession with the ears of a daughter, not those of a queer person, not even as an ally. I was already the daughter of a lesbian. Adding a trans father was more than I wanted to bear.

In an effort to mitigate your judgment, I need to explain that my father was an admitted sex addict. I couldn't tell whether this was a fetish or an identity. Was he a man who dressed a woman for sexual humiliation? Nothing was lower in his estimation than a female.

It's important to note that my father has never had boundaries when it came to his sex life. I had long been a target of his roving gaze. I've been witness and confidant beyond what a father should expect of a daughter. I am always (mostly) obedient. Or I was back then. Even when I didn't want to be.

My father has paired me with his wife or mistress in many a compare-and-contrast study on what makes a good woman, used me for a punchline in dirty jokes, told me the status of his hard-ons.

My father advised me on how to be desirable:
- have pretty hair and be good in bed,
- be smart, but don't henpeck.
- Make a healthy dinner,
- laugh at dirty jokes,
- turn the other way when the mistress walks into church,
- never say no, I'm uncomfortable, that's not funny, I don't like that.

How could I trust that his confession was pure, and that he wasn't just trying to find a way to discuss lacy underwear with me? I couldn't see if there was leer on his face over the telephone lines.

Already he showed me his wife's bras when I visited one summer, discussing their merits with me—something his wife and I both wished he wouldn't do. He showed me how he ironed them with spray starch to give her more support. Already he drew breasts on the toy rubber ducky that perched on the edge of his bathtub.

He was the kind of father who liked to push the boundaries of acceptable behavior. He said how people reacted told him everything he needed to know to understand them. I'm still not sure what that means.

The worst of it is I used my father as a punchline, a way to get sympathy, to one-up someone in bar games of Family Dysfunction Battleship. Even as I was his sole confidante. He wrote me long emails about passing at bars in fishing villages and flirting with men. My father asked me to call her Cleella and then a different name, Frances Victoria. I wrote letters to these names and mailed them to the clandestine out-of-town mailbox, addressing the envelope with only the name of the fishing boat he'd traded our beloved sailboat in for: F.V. Assiduous. My father pronounced it *assy-do-us*. I was supposed to laugh. I didn't.

When I was a child, my father signed his letters "Clint" and I only ever wanted him to be Daddy. I didn't want to see my father other than in relationship to me—we were only ever tenuously connected. The one thing he could give me that no one else could was a ticket to StraightLand. I paraded him out (metaphorically, he was never in town) to boyfriends' parents my whole life. *See? My father is straight. My father is a doctor. My father is smart and successful and my genes aren't tainted.*

But of course my genes were tainted. Even before he said he was trans my genes were never going to behave properly. I was never entirely straight, conventional, tamed. Though I was pretty good at acting as if I was.

I need to insert here that my father never changed pronouns—never used she/her. Dad only left the house dressed and made up rarely, and just when out of town. He only told his biological children and a spare niece, who happened to be a lesbian. I am uncomfortable about my use of pronouns in this essay, but *father* is a role in my life and I reject its association with gender. Father is not mother, is not friend. *Father* cannot be undone, unclaimed. And Frances V. was the one who taught me how to sail, how to build a boat, how to rewire a lamp, how to taxidermy animals—all the Daddy things—no matter what name or pronouns I use.

Does it mitigate my offense if I tell you that I didn't shame my father (I don't think) and helped F.V. pick a better wig (not that she listened) and told F.V. how and where to buy makeup? Pre-online shopping, we spent months mailing glossy catalogs back and forth between Alaska and Kansas, where I was living at the time. There was no one else to help, and Dad needed all the help I could give. I sent F.V. my best corset—the brand all my drag queen friends wore, that cost $140 at a time when that was all my spending money for two months. I always wished I had kept it for myself. I've gone soft around the middle. I'd like to wear it right now, as I write this. This corset might tame me into a better version of myself—one more restrained, more winsome, one who doesn't giggle in the wrong places. *Jiggle* I meant but *guffaw* is a better word for what I need to do less of. I've never been very good at being a girl. If I could be a better girl I might also become a better daughter.

My father shined golden rays of adoration on my brother because as son he had the right genitals. It didn't matter that

I was braver, more obedient, better in school. *A boy needs a father* and all that bullshit. It took me years to learn how, but I can pee standing up too, not that I would do it in front of my father. Now that my father no longer wants to pee standing up I don't know how I am supposed to gain his affection.

It's important to note that my father loved women as objects. My father loved men for everything else. My father adored my boyfriends and husbands and wrote them letters and sent them gifts, even after we broke up. Even as my mailbox remained empty.

Suppose I tell you that after each of my divorces my father asked me if I were a lesbian. When I said no, he replied, "Thank you. That's my biggest fear. That you will be a lesbian like your mother."

Does this person get to call themselves a lesbian trapped in a man's body?

Thank you for not being a lesbian like your mother.

Does that lessen my crime?

My father didn't get to walk into my world—the queer world—as someone who thought it would be a lark. My moms and brother and I had been here for decades. It had cost all of us something. It wasn't an identity to put on as casually as my father pulled the black miniskirt over unshaven legs.

Will you forgive me if I tell you that I was queer enough to help my father hide from his Catholic wife, who explicitly told him that this was grounds for divorce? I sincerely attempted to help. I spoke to transmen and confronted my own inner-disparager and tried my hardest to embrace this identity. I hoped that it might make everything better between us. But my father put Frances away when his wife demanded it. I was left in the closet beside her.

Now my father has dementia, or at least senility. The doctors said Alzheimer's, the doctors said Parkinson's. The wife in question insists he's fine but he can't be left alone, can no longer understand cell phones, is easily lost and confused. My father wears only what the wife in question buys and washes, folds and puts away. I don't know if Frances is still inside my father, ignored and unseen. I don't know how to say that I remember her, that despite everything, I wanted to love her, though she only existed to me in emails, in phone calls, in brown envelopes sent through the mail.

I remember, I wonder, I want

I remember my father chasing me around the playground in his red-and-black checked Woolrich coat. The Anchorage playground was chilly, even in summer. The sparse grass was dry green with brown tips, the ground mostly hard-packed dirt.

"Yaaar! It's the tickle monster!" Dad yelled and I squealed in glee. I zigged and he zagged around the monkey bars. His fingers scratched the air in tickle motions, and this made me collapse in giggling anticipation. I always let him catch me, then struggled to get away, as tickling was joy with an edge of pain. I preferred the imaginary tickle fingers to the reality. Sometimes he tickled too hard, or too long—his affection often came with an edge to it—but still. My father. On the playground. Chasing me and laughing. Like there was nowhere else he wanted to be. Like I was loved.

I remember Dad and I playing chess with his hand-carved Japanese chess set made of jade. I had a habit of knocking over the fragile pieces.

"The next time someone knocks over a piece, we're putting the game away," Dad warned me.

I didn't knock over the next piece—he did. Dad apologized as he quit playing and put the pieces in their fabric-lined case. We had to follow the rules, even though it wasn't my fault this time. I understood he was trying to teach me about fairness and treating things nicely and that he had backed himself into a corner he couldn't get out of. I ran my fingertip over the queen with her flowing robe and I didn't want her to break either. We played again the next day. He bought me a travel chess set with magnetic pieces in a case that zipped shut, but I rarely played back home in New York. Chess was only for my father.

I remember the roll and sway of Dad's sailboat, the Ghost, my father standing steady in the cockpit. He didn't bother to wipe away the rain running down his face.

"There's no point," he said, not unhappily.

I wonder if each drop kept him in the moment, if he wanted to commit this experience to memory, file away the tactile sensation alongside the harsh cry of the seagulls, the salty tang of the air. Or maybe he was resigned to the futility of wiping away rain and accepted it stoically in an effort to role-model what kind of person he wanted me to become—someone unaffected by the elements, someone whose feet stood firmly even while not on solid ground.

I remember the clammy feel of my sweatshirt against my back as I sat under the dodger at the rear of the sailboat, attempting to stay dry as I kept Dad company in the rain. Somehow, neither the damp nor the chill bothered me that day, not like it would back home in New York.

THE TRUTH ABOUT UNRINGING PHONES

When I did descend the ladder to the boat's interior, everything was warm, glowing wood. The Ghost had oval portholes with brass trimmings, a brass handrail turned green by the briny air, and a shiny brass clock that rang out four-hour shifts. The galley's stove floated like a ball compass or a Weebles toy, swaying gently with the rocking of the boat so that the surface stayed level. A small fence went around the burners in case of sudden swells. The sink had two water sources—fresh and salt. We washed the dishes with salt water, pumped with a foot petal, and only used fresh for the final rinse. The refrigerator was inside the counter and accessed by pulling up a hatch with a round, brass pull. It smelled like sour milk, and I avoided opening it if I could help it. More food was stored down in the bilge, so the coolness of the deep water kept it fresh. There was always a little seawater washing around.

The middle of the boat had two built-in benches with white cushions, and it was there that my brother, Matt, and I slept. The benches had hammock sidewalls that could be roped up to a rail at the ceiling, but we mostly didn't use them after the first day or two of sleeping at sea unless Dad told us the waves would be rough—it was too much work to put them up and take them down every day, and we were lazy, but also proud of our ability to fall into the rhythm of the sailboat, even in our sleep. Behind the cushions were cubby holes for our clothes and teddy bears. There were small bookshelves with rope to hold the books in place. Matt and I fell asleep each night to the distant rushing *shh* and *chaa* of waves breaking on the shore. The salt air was filled with the words of Tolkien's audiobooks played through the boat's cassette player, and magic swirled in my dreams.

I remember rowing our dinghies, the *Mist* and the *Spirit*, to shore. We had built them with our father the year before. Mine, the *Spirit*, was lavender, and Matt's was seafoam green, which wasn't really the color of sea foam at all. Prince William Sound was a gray-green tone of jade, and the waves bubbled white on the sandless beaches, the shore made of smoothed pebbles. The islands we visited seemed to be the Earth's bedrock itself, risen from the sea.

On the shore we separated and followed the stories in our heads, Matt and I each creating our own adventures, or at least I did. I was Thorin Oakenshield, I was a pirate, I was a treasure hunter. We went to shore even in a drizzle, because good weather was not to be relied on and we had a deadline made of miles and days to get to Cordova, a small fishing village where Dad was a visiting doctor, and where I recorded his patients' heights and weights in their charts, and called every patient to make sure they were on time.

I remember sobbing as Dad strapped us into the plane seats for our red-eye flight back home to our mothers' house. Sometimes we cried for only the first hour, sometimes my brother and I cried off-and-on for all of the eleven hours it took to get back home.

I remember the phone in my mom's dining room. It was black, with a rotary dial. The coiled cord was sprung from being stretched to its limits for privacy as we pulled the receiver around the corner, or under the table, out of view of our parents. The ringing phone was the starting bell of our frantic race to answer it.

"I got it!" My brother and I would yell, pushing each other out of the way to grasp the receiver. It was my friend Dawn or Liz, it was one of Matt's friends, it was someone for my mother. Only a few times a year was our father's voice at the other end, softened by the tinny static of long distance.

Maybe my dad meant to call. Maybe he stood in his office, stethoscope tucked between the buttons of his pinstriped dress shirt and picked up the receiver, one hand extended to press the buttons and he happened to glance at the clock, and doing the math of the four-hour time difference, noticed that it was too late.

Perhaps he thought, "I'll call as soon as I'm done with dictation," but then his pager buzzed, and he had to rush down to the ER, everything forgotten except the current emergency. Some kid was always swallowing a quarter and retrieving them was his specialty.

I wonder if he thought of me, as he sat in the concert hall and watched my stepsister sing with the school choir or play the clarinet. I wonder if he missed me when he taught my stepbrother to down-shift around the icy roads in Anchorage. I wonder if he ever wondered who taught me to drive.

I wonder if he thought about me at all between visits, or if this "second chance to be a father" (as he called his stepchildren) filled in all the missing spaces inside him, a new jigsaw puzzle piece that was close enough to fit. My second oldest stepsister, Tammy, after all, was only a week older than I was. My eldest stepsister and I both worked in law offices. The youngest siblings rode bikes, went to proms, and had friends spend the night just like I did—memories were interchangeable. Maybe the new family was exactly what he needed to make him whole. Maybe I was a passing thought, a smile of memory. Perhaps raising me was a job he considered more or less adequately done, something he took pride in, his fading memory blurring the edges of the gaps in the calendar—the ten months we were apart.

Now, when the phone rings and when I see his name on the caller ID, I push the button to send it to voice mail. Let's be honest—my father's name hasn't appeared on my caller ID that often in the last few years. After years of my declining calls he stopped trying. Or maybe he no longer remembers how to dial a phone.

I want to matter to my father.

I want the phone to ring and I want to answer it.

I want to *want* to answer the phone if my father ever calls me again.

I'm not sure I will.

Fragment of Yearning: Choices

In 2015 my father and Tricia left Alaska for Seattle, where Tricia's four children and my half-sister all resided within an hour's drive of each other. My father apologized to me not choosing to live closer to my brother or me, who are both on the East side of the country. For choosing them over us.

I got it. It was pragmatic.

He didn't say it, but I knew there were more of them in one location.

He didn't say it, but neither Matt nor I were the favorite child any longer.

He didn't say it, but Dad no longer made the decisions in his marriage about such things.

I didn't say it, but I didn't want to be the only child in town to take care of him.

I didn't say it, but I was planning on moving out of state soon, anyway.

I didn't say it, but I still wish he had chosen me or at least my brother.

My stepmother asked me what he'd said. I relayed his apology and she replied, "That's ridiculous—we'd never do that."

[We'd never move to be near you.]

I got it, it was pragmatic, he didn't need to say it, so why did she have to?

Dementia, 2018-2019

When I flew in for my nephew's funeral, I went to dinner with my father and his wife, Tricia, in a restaurant adjacent to a hotel in downtown Seattle. We hadn't picked it specifically, but traffic was bad and the location was handy.

"I need to go to the bathroom," my father said.

"You're wearing Depends, just go in your pants," Tricia answered. To get to the bathroom, customers had to leave the restaurant, enter the attached hotel lobby, and walk down a hall and up two steps. Parkinson's had reduced my father's once confident strides into a slow, rickety shuffle.

Ten minutes later, my father asked to go to the bathroom again, so I walked with him, like I do for my children. I waited outside for him to finish, and from my position it was obvious that it was for the benefit of the entire restaurant that he hadn't chosen to go in his pants.

After dinner, my father and I waited for Tricia to retrieve the car.

"Do you know how to remember the main streets of Seattle?" he asked.

I did not, since I'd only been to Seattle a handful of times.

"Jesus Christ Made Seattle Under Pressure," he crowed. "That's how to remember the main streets: Jefferson and

James, Cherry and Columbia, Marion and Madison, Spring and Seneca, University and Union, then Pike and Pine Streets."

I made impressed noises, but I didn't care. A homeless man approached us, and I told him we had no cash. A group of young men headed for a Pearl Jam concert passed us by in the darkening evening, then more and more people crowded the sidewalks. The crowd was expected to number over 40,000. My father used to be the strongest person I knew, but I was now keenly aware that if anything happened, it was up to me to defend my father. I tightened my hand into a fist. I took aerobic kickboxing, lifted light weights. I didn't know if any of that would be useful, but I was all we had as the city sank into dusk.

Dad and I struggled with small talk as we waited. After fifteen minutes, Tricia called and explained that she had lost the parked car but thought she'd find it soon. More time went on, and my father became agitated.

"Call her. Tell her we are on the corner of Cherry. Remind her that Jesus Christ Made Seattle Under Pressure," he repeated. I explained that Tricia knew where we were, it was the car she was having trouble locating. "Tell her Jesus Christ Made Seattle Under Pressure," he insisted. He was near tears, so I called his wife and had her calm him down. Tricia eventually found the car and picked us up.

In December, 2019, my stepsister, Tammy, asked Juli to ask Matt and me how much money we could contribute to our father's care. My father had chosen Tammy to be his power of attorney, executor, everything. If it came down to pulling the plug on life support, she was the person to make that decision. None of the Lillibridge children had a voice in our father's care, but that was how he wanted it. Matt and I waivered, but our spouses were adamantly opposed to sending anything. Vehemently opposed.

"Fuck that," said my sister-in-law, who is the kindest person in the family. I didn't know she knew the word fuck.

The stepsister who communicates with me sounds burdened by having to deal with my father. It is not my fault he chose them to bear the weight of his care. My father left Alaska to be Grandpa down the street to their children. There is no place for me in my father's life, except when they want something, like money, which I do not send.

I'd like to make a list of all the reasons he should choose me over my stepsisters—why he should spend holidays and weekends with my children but there are no words that will move him. His new family gives him comfort. That should be enough for me.

My father was in the hospital for dehydration. No one was exactly sure why. I called the hospital under pressure from Juli and spoke to him.

"They forgot my medicine for Type 2 Diabetes," he complained.

"You don't have Type 2 Diabetes, Dad. Tricia does," I said.

"I've had it for twenty years!"

I gave up. "How do you feel today, Dad?"

"We're gonna win!"

Tricia had a stroke at the end of November, 2019. She lay crumbled on the living room floor. Dad could not lift her, could not figure out how to call for help, or maybe he forgot she was there. Kym told me Tricia lay on the floor for twelve hours.

"We don't blame Clint, but…" she said. If I were her, I wouldn't be able to refrain from blame, no matter that my mind knew he had dementia.

"Sis, he thought she was dead," Juli explained to me. "He thought Tricia was dead and he couldn't remember how to use the cell phone. He has nightmares about it still."

Dad moved in with Juli for a few months. He ate an entire tub of margarine with a spoon for breakfast, put his Depends on the outside of his pants, and mistook Juli for her mother, thinking it was date night. Eventually, he was reunited with his wife in an assisted living facility. Tricia had another stroke and was moved to a care facility for stroke survivors, and Dad remained three hours away in the new apartment that they only had lived together in for a few weeks. Juli asked me to call him every day to keep his spirits up. I told her to stop asking.

Yet, I couldn't stop thinking about him all alone in his new apartment. I pictured him walking down the hall, pausing at the front door, reading the sign reminding him to stay inside. I remind myself that I am not obligated to take care of a man who abandoned me over and over. It is not my fault that he's lonely. But it feels like it is.

The cry of gulls and smell of salt water as Dad read *The Hobbit* to us aloud. Dad's copy was dated January, 1973—nearly ten years old.

"We must have bought this on the trip when we conceived you," Dad told me. I looked down and said nothing, not wanting to think of Dad and Mom having sex on vacation.

The boat rolled gently side-to-side as my father read, then made Matt and I each take turns reading aloud. He taught me to take notes in books, to underline, to make a book into a marker in time to remind us of who we were at that moment.

To be in my father's presence was to feel the full beam of his attention, like the way sunlight looks coming in a window—my brother and I were the dust particles dancing and glistening under his gaze, finally magical. Finally beautiful.

When I left his line of sight, I was forgotten in darkness, ordinary dust once more. And someone else—some other woman's children—got to feel his warmth. Whether they wanted to or not made little difference.

Juli asks me to call him again. "He is so lonely," she implores.

I look at my phone, my fingers itch, clench, release. I don't call my father.

An Illustrative Example

I loved the Anchorage airport. Glass cases held taxidermy animals: moose, and a giant polar bear standing on its hind legs. Normally, I walked out of the jet way, and Dad was right there. Sometimes Matt and I had to walk to the end of the terminal to find him, but the airport was small. When I was somewhere between nine and twelve, I flew to Alaska alone, which wasn't unusual. Our winter visits were often "alone time" with Dad. What was unusual was that Dad wasn't at the end of the jet way, nor in the main terminal, nor at baggage claim.

It was ok, though. I knew the procedure. I stood at the conveyor belt, watching for my blue Samsonite suitcase. When I saw it, I pulled it off one-handed, then moved to a corner to wait for Dad. Just like a grown up.

> How much longer
> How much longer
> How much longer

I had looked at the calendar with longing for months and waited and waited to see him again, and I counted every excruciatingly long hour on every excruciatingly long flight and every excruciatingly long lay over, watching the hour hand move me closer to Dad as the time zones moved me farther from my mother until she and I were four hours apart and now Dad and I were minutes away from each other. But minutes piled up and turned into hours and still he did not come. All the passengers from my flight left, and then another flight's worth of baggage circled on the conveyor belt, and still I waited. I couldn't see the polar bear or any of the other animals from my perch on my battered and duct taped suitcase, but I didn't wander off to look at them. I didn't read a book. I just scanned the crowd for my father's beard and black sea captain's hat.

> How much longer
> How much longer
> How much longer

Eventually an airport employee tapped me on the shoulder and wanted to know who I was waiting for. I gave her Dad's name, but I didn't know his office number or the name of his practice, but she was resourceful and knew someone who knew someone and was able to track him down after a few calls.

He'd forgotten I was coming that day.

I didn't understand because I had spoken to him the night before. We always called the night before, to make sure everything was arranged, just like I had practiced calling Mom collect, to make sure I knew how to do it in case of emergency. (Of course this wasn't an emergency, so I hadn't called her. I was sure Dad would come.)

I didn't understand that he hadn't been counting the days, hours, or minutes between us.

I didn't understand that my love for my father was like balancing my small body on a teeter-totter against his larger weight—I was always floating, leaning back, squirming to make something work on my own, when all I needed was for him to put one foot down to keep us in balance.

To Survive I Sold my Truth.

In counseling when I was fifteen, I was given the phrase, "covert sexual abuse" to describe my father's actions. He didn't have to touch me; it didn't have to be worse than it was. It was still wrong. It was still trauma.

I used these words when speaking to my father's wife at the time, Teresa, #6, who told my father, who called me up the night before I was scheduled to visit him and told me I was a liar—a lying little snot, to be precise—he was never sexually abusive. The phone was beige with brown buttons. It plugged into a jack in my parents' bedroom, but the cord was long enough to stretch across the hall to my room.

"I'm not the one who will stand in judgement for this," I said, my heart racing, my hands slick against the plastic telephone receiver, using the words of the new religion I had joined.

"Maybe you will," my brother said, who was living with our father at the time.

I hadn't known that Dad had asked him to pick up an extension. I hung up on both of them.

I didn't speak to my father for a year. I refused to mail back the plane ticket when my mother asked, even though it cost over one thousand dollars. I didn't give her the ticket the second or third time she asked either, but I didn't throw it away. I wanted him to have to pay some penalty. Looking at the ticket made my stomach burn, but in that anger was also pride. I was holding him accountable, even though my mother—who was usually my ally—didn't support my punishment.

Matt and I didn't speak of it, but I understood. He was living with Dad. We were teenagers. What else could he have done? I know he knew the truth of our childhood. That was enough to loosen my rage at his betrayal.

At seventeen I moved out of my moms' house, and I needed that child support check from my dad—to have a place to live I had to sell my truth. I called my father from my boyfriend's house and told him I lied. I needed the money to live, and I didn't know how else to get it. I didn't understand he was legally obligated to send it whether we were speaking or not. I didn't understand divorce law. Dad asked me to apologize every time I spoke to him for the next few years, and every time I did, I hated myself for selling out. Every time I recanted, my outer shell hardened, my remembered child-self grew desiccated and slowly turned to dust.

Liminal Space of 30,000 Feet

Flying to Alaska was our transition between Mom and Pat, and Dad. It was our decompression chamber, our acclimation to the next house—no, it was a state of suspended animation between the two houses. An emptiness filled only with waiting.

One hour and forty-five minutes to Chicago. Five hours to Seattle. Another two and a half hours to Alaska. An hour or two or sometimes three at each airport in-between. All told, it took eleven hours on average to see our father, and another eleven to return home to our moms.

The day my brother and I spent flying to Alaska—unaccompanied, belonging only to each other—we occupied a liminal space between parents, between rules, between the queer, female-dominated world of Mom and Pat's house and Dad's male-centered, heterosexual and overly-sexual household. At Mom's house, I was the unacknowledged favorite, the responsible one, the bossy one. In Alaska, my brother reigned supreme. We boarded our first flight in Rochester as equals, but at each airport, Matt pulled ahead. He navigated the airports without maps, and I was afraid to be without him. He led me through the rainbow tunnel in O'Hare or down to SEA-TAC's subway, and he always knew which way to go. By the time we landed in Alaska, I was solidly in his shadow, where I'd remain all summer.

DC-10s were my favorite planes. Huge, with multiple segments, five seats across the middle, two more on each side. Once, we were on a plane with a spiral staircase to the first-class lounge on the second floor. When no one was looking, Matt and I tried to creep up the stairs to take a peek. We got caught and returned to our seats in coach.

We flew in 1970s planes with fabric curtains on the windows. Every seat got at least one blanket and pillow. Once, during the air traffic control strike of 1981, we flew in a cargo plane with our father. We sat sideways against the wall, and they gave us each a cardboard box with lunch inside. It was too loud to talk but the food was better than regular airplane meals. I don't know how Daddy got us on that plane—he was in the Air Force very briefly (discharged for bleeding disorder) but officer's ID cards never expire, and he wasn't afraid to pull a rank he never properly earned.

I hated the honey-roasted peanuts every flight attendant handed out on commercial flights. The meals were horrible except for dessert, but one year Mom (or Dad) learned that they could request a children's meal. It didn't always work—sometimes our parents forgot or the plane people forgot. But sometimes the flight attendant brought us our own special trays as if we were movie stars, and beneath the lid was a bag of chips, a steaming hot dog or hamburger, and a cookie.

We never really had enough money for headsets for movies, and if we did, it was a hard choice whether spend it or save it for candy. If there were no headsets on the seat when we boarded, that meant there would be a movie. If there was a headset, that flight only had music. Generally, each music channel had a rotation of the same 8 or 10 songs played on every flight on the way there and back again. Sometimes I chewed on the headset—the bottom end was two-pronged ribbed plastic, not rigid, but with some give to it. Chewing on it was all it was good for.

We boarded the plane with books to read and the flight attendants always gave us a deck of cards, but the novelty of everything wore off after a few hours. Looking out the window, I'd picture jumping on the cloud layer as if it were a trampoline, or sinking into it as if it were down, but imaginings could only occupy me for so long. Matt and I pushed the call button over and over to summon the increasingly irritated flight attendant.

Bing. Are we there yet?
Bing. How much longer?
Bing. My brother did…my sister said…
Bing.
Bing.
Bing.
We had a coke-drinking competition. We read books, we poked each other and fought, we slept. We cried.

Leaving Alaska, we always cried. Sometimes for an entire flight, sometimes for all three of the flights home. Sometimes with heaving shoulders and noises drowned out by the plane's engines. Sometimes only on the inside—sitting frozen, not reading, not looking out the window. The sadness deep in my bones—my ribs, my lungs, my hips.

It's Not as if My Father Did Nothing for Me

When my first husband was in a severe motorcycle accident, Dad and Tricia sent us $2,000 to help with the bills—not as a loan but as a gift. Dad paid $140 a session for my counseling even after I was married and no longer his legal burden. He paid for a marriage retreat for my first husband and me to try and save our dysfunctional marriage.

Dad paid for the first three years of my college, per the divorce agreement: tuition, books, living expenses. He continued to pay my tuition even after I got married at twenty— until I dropped out the first time. I did not ask him to contribute when I returned to college a few years later.

He paid for my first divorce, on Tricia's condition that I get an annulment, so I could get married again in the Catholic Church. I never followed through with the annulment because I wasn't Catholic, though I agreed to sign the document when my ex-husband asked me so that he could get married again. (He never followed up.)

When I got divorced the first time, Dad helped me retrieve my belongings from New York and move them to Florida.

They sent me gifts for Christmas, my birthday, my kids' birthdays. Cards on holidays. Most years I got a mention in the Xmas newsletter—not every year, but with more regularity than Matt or Juli.

It is more than many people get. Why doesn't it feel like enough?

Escape from New York

My first husband and I were in marriage counseling. I had myself promised I would never divorce, never follow in my father's footsteps of marriage after marriage after marriage. I didn't want to fulfill everyone's expectations of what a Lillibridge was—I didn't want to *be* a Lillibridge. I had made my bed, and I was going to lie in it even if I burned to ashes as I lie there, but after my husband screamed at me in front of the counselor and stormed out of the session, she told me, "Don't go home. Women are most likely to be killed when they try to leave. Just get in your car and drive to your mother's in Florida."

It wasn't even the bad kind of screaming like he did at home, just what I thought of as a regular amount of screaming. I was surprised she thought it was bad enough to leave, but it was the permission I had been waiting for.

I went to the bank first and took out cash, but I didn't empty the account. I wanted to be fair. I hid the envelope in the trunk, next to my rollerblades.

I couldn't leave my pets. I knew she told me not to go home, but I just couldn't leave them. I drove home, and the three dogs were outside. I put my favorite, a Rottweiler named Anubis, in the backseat of my car, and let the other two dogs into the house. I found my favorite cat, Persephone, in the living room and quietly took her outside and slipped her into the front seat of the old Toyota I had borrowed from my mother after my own was totaled in an accident the month before. I had already decided to take the two female cats and leave the males—not out of sexism, but because the males roamed the neighborhood and I knew they could take care of themselves. The females needed regular food and litter box cleaning—something that my husband had never done. The plan had been forming for months now, I just hadn't had the courage to act on it. My hands shook and when I looked at my chest, I could see my heart pounding as I went upstairs to where I had hidden two suitcases with my favorite summer clothes. I still had to find the other cat.

"What are you doing, Lara?" he asked through the closed door. I had never heard him sound so devoid of emotion. I knew he had four guns in the room with him: a 12 gauge, a 30-30, a black semi-automatic, and a black powder revolver. He always said, "I'd never hurt you, because I love you too much."

I couldn't trust that was still true.

I left the suitcases, left the other cat, grabbed my jewelry box—the only thing I had to pawn—and ran down the stairs and out the door. I fumbled with my car door, afraid to look back and see if he was following. I turned right at the end of the street, my tires squealing, and clipped the curb in my haste. 490 to the turnpike. 90 to Pittsburgh. I was free.

Pat, my mom's partner, met me in Pennsylvania, and she and I drove the rest of the way down to Key West together. Mom and Pat took me in until I found a job and a place of my own. They paid off my credit card debt, took me to their church and introduced me to all their friends. They gave me a community and introduced me to a gay boy who became my best friend. Their neighbor donated clothing to me, and I shopped at the Salvation Army and K-Mart. Eventually my ex allowed my moms to move my things into a storage unit, where the boxes sat for a year. I sent my check from Key West to Rochester month after month, an amount equal to half my rent, until my father swept in with a plan to help me. I didn't ask, he just saw what needed to be done and did it, like a good parent.

The Right Tap

I had forgotten how warm the water is straight out of the faucet in Key West. Open the cold tap, and you'll get water warm enough to bathe in. The water comes down a pipe one hundred and sixty miles from Miami, solar warm under the hot sun, saturated with dissolved makeup they used to say, or pipe rust or medication probably. I drank it anyway and didn't mind at all.

Cold hurts my soul. Winter always left me immobile-frozen to the sidewalk, eyebrows stinging needles, cold ache in my bones, fingers and toes blanched pale yellow. When it's cold, people cut you off in traffic and they don't have enough energy left to say hello to strangers, because all their molecules are busy with keeping the body warm. It's not their fault. We are all ice frozen. Our insides need to thaw to let the goodness out.

But not here. Here the tap water greets you with warmth as your brush your teeth. Here is where I came when I walked out of my life, got in the car and drove until the road ended. Driving is healing, singing Gloria Gaynor to drown out the cat crying in the backseat, eating soggy egg sandwiches on hamburger buns you bought at Wal-Mart along with some

THE TRUTH ABOUT UNRINGING PHONES

Hanes Her Way because you left everything back in New York except your pets and rollerblades. Driving to beat blizzards and driving through snow as far south as the Carolinas. It was a hard winter that year you escaped, a hard life you had to lead.

Sometimes crazy is a decision. Sometimes you are on the brink of it and can fall off either way, and if you straddle the limbo life will choose your descent for you. Sometimes you flirt with crazy and let it flow in waves over your feet beach-style, and a rip tide carries you out farther than you intended. And crazy is contagious. Sometimes when crazy is winning in your household you have to run away before it jumps on your back and digs its claws into your flesh, renting gashes in your skin.

Sometimes you don't run soon enough and you'll carry those scars for a while but they will fade. Trust me, the mahogany lines turn pink then silver and in years to come you'll look down and be surprised that you can still see them, and surprised that they aren't darker.

One day I drove and drove stick-shift car no cruise control four days. My dog cat stepmother riding along radio blaring *I Will Survive*. I drove through fear, it ebbed like the snow as I got further south. His angry bald head—open mouth always yelling shooting rubber bb guns at the dogs and a handgun in the backyard road rage anger management and too many prescription drugs—it all receded in my wake until I couldn't picture it clearly anymore. A good road trip will do that for you. I didn't have to be the sacrificial lamb to the promise I gave in church to stay until death did we part, which seemed to be just over the horizon. Mine anyway. I got in the old car, borrowed from my mother, the same model as the first one I ever drove, and the light blue interior worn-out seats rusted doors windup windows helped rewind me to who I had once been. I owned that car when I met him.

It seemed fitting that in spite of all the new cars that came after, I left in the same model I drove in with. I got in that car with my rollerblades and my favorite cat and one huge Rottweiler and five thousand dollars hidden in the trunk—my security, emptied from the bank right before it closed. I left him most of the money from the house fire insurance check, only taking enough to escape and pay the bills in my name. The road unraveled the ribbons of who I used to be until they fluttered free in the car's wake. The spool unwound until it was empty and I was ready to be wound in something new, wrapped up with who I yearned to be.

I pulled up in the driveway ten miles from the end of the road and the sky was filled with thoughts and stars. The air warm on my skin, all my skin and hair was warm even my toes and fingertips. And the cold-water faucet sent me more warm water.

I got a job, got a house, got friends, moved again and again and again and through all of it I was glad. I worked hot steaming gift shops with no air conditioning into the dark of tourist winter and I was not too hot.

THE TRUTH ABOUT UNRINGING PHONES

    I did not crave winter or seasons or tulips as much as I craved night blooming jasmine and bougainvillea and lizards running from my feet on the hot sidewalk like mice. The things that I craved I was given here over and over, and other things I did not know I needed, like a church I didn't believe in but loved to attend and bingo at a gay bar and drag queens with sparkly pink lips. A gay roommate who chose my shoes and borrowed my clothes and taught me to watch *The Golden Girls* in bed after work, sometimes with wine even though he was underage, but just barely.

I got a boyfriend then another husband I thought I wanted and said I'd move north even though I had given away all my winter clothes because I had sworn that I was not going back, never. I was not crazy mad in love with him, but he glowed with a halo that was probably just his red hair in the streetlight, but it was easy to mistake it for destiny. We never fought, and he was looking ahead in the same direction I was, and I knew I couldn't trust my heart to make good choices and I knew where crazy love got me before, so I knew I was better off without it.

We married in secret and this seemed to be the right path, so I quit my job, quit my life, quit my island, and packed the trunk with a thousand tiny bags and brought that same cat back off the island with me. The dog had been buried two years before. We got in my little red car and I took down my sparkling drag queen fish that hung off my rearview mirror because he said I had to, and if it had to be done I would bury my own, not leave him to do it for me.

It turned out that looking in the same direction wasn't enough to base a life on, and I found in the end I could not live without that fish hanging from my rearview mirror. Five years later I hung it in my car once again, though the two-door red coupe was now a gold minivan filled with children's car seats, and this time I drove across town, not across the country.

I had my talisman fish but I couldn't go back south. Sometimes things can't be undone and this was one of them. And I stayed north where water flows cold from the cold tap and snow falls from gray clouds on gray sidewalks.

But not always. There is summer and beaches and sunshine and you forget that it isn't always like this until September slaps your face with hard cold reality and you can't drag summer out even one more day though you beg and plead with the sky. And you say this year it won't be so bad in winter and by and by it is not that bad anymore in winter.

Then one day you come back south for two moons and a day and you don't remember streets or people's names and you're a tourist not a local in what once felt like your hometown. And you realize you've lived north thirty-seven years and south only three, so why do you hang on to it as the place you were meant to live, when you were just a flash in the island's pan of revolving residents fried in oil served with a plantain? You turn on the cold tap and warm water floods your hands and then it all comes back how the island loved you and always gave you what you needed.

THE TRUTH ABOUT UNRINGING PHONES

And the faucet is shaped like Aladdin's lamp, unexpectedly bulbous, but it is granting you this wish, a promise that you can return. A promise that the warm Key West water that came all the way down the pipe from Miami will be waiting for your hands.

Moving My Stuff

My father flew from Alaska to New York with a canvas bag of tools—this was pre-9/11, when a hammer wasn't considered a weapon. He emptied out my storage units and loaded the Penske rental truck as I flew north from Florida, then he picked me up at the airport and we headed down the road to Key West after a one-night stop to visit my brother.

I-95 unrolled before us, the sun glinting off the hairline cracks in the windshield. The gray seats didn't recline, but there was plenty of legroom. It wasn't as uncomfortable as I thought it would be.

I was grateful to him and afraid of being alone together for 1,800 miles. I didn't want to spend a week having close personal conversations. I needed my belongings—my photographs and clothing, the furniture handed down to me by my mother when I had first moved out, my childhood teddy bears—all the tangible bits of memories I had accumulated in my twenty-seven years—and had no other means of getting them. I couldn't afford to retrieve them on my own. Dad and I still had a relationship then—I had seen him and Tricia a year before, and we'd had a nice visit, but when he hugged me, I couldn't feel it. My walls were too thick, the distance between who we actually were to each other and who we were pretending to be for a week was too great for me to breach. But alone on the road hour after uninterrupted hour foisted an unavoidable level of intimacy on us that I wanted to duck out from under, the way I ducked out of his hugs when they went on too long.

Things I didn't want to talk about:
- How I accused him of sexual abuse in high school and then recanted, then wished I could un-recant but didn't know how.
- His parenting mistakes and my forgiveness for them.
- Anything about the past.
- David and Dale, Juli's half-brothers on her mother's side, who were of no relationship to me, and yet Dad insisted were "my brothers." One of them molested Juli, one did his best to defend her. One came drunk to Juli's wedding, and one I met in Alaska when I was fourteen and I didn't like him. I honestly have no idea which brother is which. David-n-Dale, like Laranme, another sibling set my sister was not included in.

Other things I wanted to avoid:
- Dirty jokes.
- Comments about his sex life.
- Seeing each other naked.

"Lara-lara!" he called at the airport curb, smooshing me against his chest in too hard of a hug. His stubble scratched my forehead. He smelled like old wool and Dad. I wanted to hug him back, melt my defensive shield, but I didn't know how to dismantle my shell. I patted his back awkwardly. I both was excited to see him, and not.

I climbed into the truck cab and he pointed out the red plastic urinal.

"I got this so we wouldn't have to stop to pee!" he said.

"I'm not peeing in that, Dad," I said.

"Oh."

He handed me *Harry Potter,* a book he'd gifted to me twice before and I had not been able to get through. I sighed. I was not interested in *Harry Potter.*

"I thought we could read it aloud as we drive," Dad said.

"I get sick when I read in the car," I countered.

"Oh. Well, I'll just read to you then."

"OK, but no character voices." Dad loved to change his voice. It creeped me out. More than that, though, was that it was something I could take away from him. I couldn't stop him from reading and I couldn't choose the book, but I could at least make it a little less enjoyable for him, and a little less disturbing for me. I wasn't able to make myself act as a good daughter. Dad was determined to make everything work.

It turned out, I loved *Harry Potter,* and reading the book filled in all the empty spaces left by the conversations we were avoiding. We decided together how to pronounce Hermione, which was a nice way of Dad telling me I was saying it wrong.

THE TRUTH ABOUT UNRINGING PHONES

We read and chatted about the book all the way down the coast, stopping to spend the night at the Omega Institute to visit my brother, who worked there, and somewhere in the Carolinas to see a friend of Dad's from Alaska. I introduced Dad to Cracker Barrel, and we ate dinner at a different one every night.

The drive was sunny, pleasant, the days didn't feel endlessly long. It was an unexpectedly happy memory, and none of the topics I was dreading came up in conversation.

I needed help, and he swept in and saved me. The way the fathers always do in Hallmark movies.

We hit the Florida coast on Memorial Day weekend. Up until then, motels were easy to find, but neither of us had foreseen that driving down the seaside on a holiday weekend was a bad idea. It got later and later as we tried hotel after hotel. We had cell phones but not smart ones, and I fumbled with the map and called directory assistance for phone numbers of hotels in the next town, then the next one. Finally, at 10:00pm, we found a place with a single room and a king-sized bed. It was that or sleep in the truck, and the seats didn't recline. Dad left it up to me, and I agreed to share the bed. We both slept in our clothes and surprisingly, I fell asleep easily and slept all night.

The next day we made it to Key West. We unloaded the truck and spent the day sightseeing. I took him on the Western Union—a restored tall wooden ship. He drove the truck alone four hours back to Miami to return it and rented a car and drove back down to Key West without complaint. He gave me a hug that night in the living room, wearing a T-shirt that ended at his navel. No pants. No underwear. He was back to being who he had always been.

The next day my live-in boyfriend called me at work.

"I was sleeping and your dad walked into our bedroom without knocking. He was stark naked. He wanted to know where his toiletry bag was."

"I'm not capable of getting my father to wear pants. I've tried and failed my whole life."

But that wasn't true—the only trying I'd done was via sending mental signals and pained expressions. I was incapable of telling him he was inappropriate. I couldn't confront him and risk what little relationship we had.

Fragment of Yearning: Hope

I am afraid if I open my father wounds I will bleed out. It is easier to tell the stories that scarred me than the ones that brought me joy. Happy reminisces breed hope, and hope scrapes away my resolve, reveals my soft, vulnerable underbelly. That has never worked well for me when it comes to my father.

LARA LILLIBRIDGE

Don't Give Baby Birds to Children to Raise

Dad and Margaret, his fourth wife, bought fourteen acres of land on Lake Louise in "the bush." Dad named it Loon Landing and set up eight tent camping sites on the top of a gravel hill that overlooked the lake. Dad hated RV's and discouraged them, but I could tell it would be an unpleasant, rocky place to pitch a tent, and people didn't do it very often.

Down at the bottom of the lake, where no campers were allowed to go, there were four cabins. Closest to the lake was the Taylor cabin, where Dad and Margaret slept. It had all the food, and we ate sitting in a straight row at a counter, looking out at the water. Next was the Lillibridge Cabin, where Matt and I were locked in every night, and beyond that was the King cabin, where Juli and our then stepsister Anne slept. They were both sixteen so no one had to lock them in.

Across the hill from the King cabin was the guest cabin, and if one of Margaret's other daughters came to visit, that's where they stayed. The lake had a half-sunk pontoon boat but no dock. We had three canoes, and a few outbuildings. I think the plan was to repair the lodge and open it to campers someday. Dad was always building something in it though. He built a boat and we had a naming contest. Everyone in the family put names into a jar and Margaret pulled one out. She picked Juli's name, "The Jewel," and so Juli got to smash the bottle of champagne on the hull to christen it before its maiden voyage.

Dad always made a production like that. Once I found a dead vole, and I was so sad that this tiny adorable creature died, so Dad had a funeral for it. He scheduled it in the afternoon so everyone could dress up. Margaret wore her best green satin dress with the jewel tone pattern that reached her toes. Dad held a moose bone as a pretend microphone and performed the ceremony laying the vole to rest. A vole is only about two inches long, so it was probably the biggest event anyone ever had for a creature they never met while it was living. It might have been the kindest thing my father ever did for me.

The gravel crunched beneath Dad's feet as he walked to the solarium he was building, lumber carried casually on one shoulder. Dad climbed the ladder and hoisted black rolls of roofing material to me. The roll said "fifty pounds" but he lifted them easily with one hand. Dad was the strongest person I knew.

He wasn't unusually tall, only 5'10" I think, though he's shrunk since then. He was more wiry than burly. He flexed his arm and pointed to a spot below his elbow.

"Do you see that muscle?" he asked me. "That's called *the egg*. That means you are really strong." I flexed my own arm, but I had no egg. I squeezed my biceps with my fingers, but the muscle was squishy.

THE TRUTH ABOUT UNRINGING PHONES

The solarium was going to have fiberglass panels to let light in "for tanning," but in Alaska that seemed unlikely, even in summer. Since we had no electricity though, windows were essential.

Dad installed a hot tub outside the building before it was finished. It was red colored wood and smelled delicious. "It's a hot tub, because it doesn't have jets. Jacuzzi's have jets," he explained. We sat in the tub together in our underwear. I was wearing my best underwear—Strawberry Shortcake Days of the Week bikinis—the only high cut panties I owned, but I was embarrassed because I was wearing the wrong day of the week since I only had three pair. I got into the steaming water quickly so no one would notice.

I'm not sure now why we were wearing underwear since we were generally nude all the time. A plane flew low overhead, and Dad told us to hide under the water.

One day when Dad was fixing the lodge roof he knocked off a sparrow's nest, which was made of mud and adhered to the side of the building under the roof's overhang. Dad put the four birds in a shoebox and gave them to Matt and me to raise in the Lillibridge cabin. We fed them Rice Krispies soaked in water using a little eyedropper, and they were really pushy and Matt and I often dropped the mush on the birds themselves and glued their eyes shut with it. They cried all night and we fed them over and over. We named them Thorin, Sam, Feeli and Keeli, all Hobbit names, because my Hobbit obsession had already begun. Matt was not Hobbit obsessed, but he liked Sam from *The Lord of the Rings* well enough.

Feeli and Keeli were the first to die at the feet of their siblings. As they fought for food, the larger birds stepped on the smaller ones and snapped their necks. The same fate befell Thorin, my favorite. Sam lived enough to be relocated to the Taylor cabin, where he learned to fly around a bit, but after we went home at the end of the summer, Juli's cat ate him.

Don't give baby birds to children to raise. It doesn't end well.

Down at the lake, I spent a lot of time trying to catch a minnow in a jar to keep as my pet. I wanted more pets. Juli was only allowed a cat because her mother died and so she had to move to Alaska and she brought her cat with her. Eventually the orange tabby jumped from the second story balcony of the condo and was never seen again. Dad had Chuckchi, his husky, but she was a work dog. She pulled a dog cart Dad filled with the firewood we all had had to take turns splitting with an axe. She never came inside but stayed tied to a long chain next to her doghouse. She always slept on the roof of the doghouse. I never saw her go inside it.

Margaret caught a minnow once. "It died," she told me, as an explanation for why I wasn't allowed to keep a minnow if I happened to catch one. "I gave it lettuce to eat and everything."

"I was going to collect some algae from the lake to feed my minnow," I told her.

"I never thought of that," Margaret said.

I didn't know if minnows ate algae but I knew they sure as shit didn't eat lettuce. "No wonder it died," I thought. But I was never able to catch a minnow in a jar, so it didn't matter.

Matt and I swam in the frigid lake out to the half-sunk pontoon boat. It wasn't really a boat. It was a wooden platform with two gray metal pontoons attached. Perhaps it had been a swimming platform once upon a time. But one of the pontoons was stuck to the bottom of the lake, and the wooden platform rose like the side of a mountain.

One day Matt ran down the gravel hill and fell, sliding on one knee and landing in some broken glass. Dad and Margaret had to take him to Glennallen, the nearest town, which was almost an hour away. We knew that meant he was hurt bad because the few times Matt needed stitches Dad did them himself. But the knee required an actual hospital. Matt came home with a rubber tube sewn into his knee that dripped white fluid. It was the worst thing that ever happened to either of us. A few weeks later they went back to the hospital to have the tube taken out and have the wound sewn shut.

Every cabin had a white 5-gallon bucket with a toilet seat on it, and we had a bathroom building that had stalls but only more buckets inside. People had written graffiti in the stalls a long time ago, or maybe Dad had written it himself: "If you voted for Nixon, you can't pee here. Your Dick is in Washington." Dad made Matt help him when it was time to empty the buckets. I never had to.

We also had a broken-down dump truck to play on. You could turn the steering wheel and pull the choke in and out, but the pedals were stuck to the floor and the other knobs didn't move. The back was filled with debris I sorted through looking for treasure. Matt peed off the back of the dump truck, his urine arching golden in the sun, but when I tried, my pee only went straight down.

Sometimes the whole family played kickball or soccer in the field up by the campground. There were gooseberry bushes, which looked like blueberries but were gritty and sour. I ate them anyway. We were allowed to roam freely throughout the woods, and I never knew where our woods ended and someone else's woods began.

Every night and every morning we gathered to listen to the Caribou Clatters, when the local radio station DJ read messages to people in the bush like us, without telephones or electricity. Sometimes Mom and Pat would call in with a message for Matt and me, and when we were in town, we would always call the station to send a message to whomever was still manning the campground. Dad had to work, so one week was Juli and me at Loon Landing alone, while Matt, Dad, and Margaret were in town. The next week Juli and I were in town and Matt and Margaret were alone at the camp. The third week we all were there together. I never asked Matt what happened when he and Margaret were alone. It is only now that it occurred to me that it was weird not to speak of it.

Once Matt sent Juli a message, "Say hi to Lucifer for me," when Juli and I were there alone. Juli about died because she was a good Christian girl and Lucifer meant the devil. Matt and I were not raised Christian so we thought it was a cute take on lucy-fur or something. We didn't see anything wrong with it, and why name the cat something that embarrassed you?

We drove to Loon Landing in the back of Big Mama, a white and yellow Dodge van. The seats were removed in the way back and replaced with wall-to-wall shag carpeting. Sometimes Matt and I (or one of us) got to fly with Dad in his Piper-Colt which was cool because it was only an hour trip instead of four in the van. We watched Dad do the pre-flight, checking the gas in all three tanks, and making sure it was clear and pink. Once Daddy crashed his old plane because the maintenance guys put the wrong fuel in. When we were set to go we did the final check, "Mixture full rich, carb heat cold, mags on both. Off, off, off." Dad opened the window and yelled, "Clear!" even if we were on the gravel strip without anyone else around. Then the propeller started and it was too loud to talk without yelling.

We flew over the edges of the mountains, and we saw white goats clinging to the rocky incline, or moose walking across the tundra. There were glaciers and silty water. Dad would let us take the yoke and we learned that if you got scared you only had to let go and the plane would right itself. I loved to tell my friends back in NY that I knew how to fly, I just didn't know how to take-off and land. The plane had only two seats, and if Matt was there, too, I sat on a suitcase behind them. Sometimes Dad's husky sat back there, too.

"How fast are we going?" I asked Dad.

"Oh, probably 100 miles an hour," he said, and I thought that was the fastest I had ever gone in my life.

Underwear Regrets

Saying that my father has a warped sense of humor is akin to saying that he has blue eyes—if you have been in a room with him for more than ten minutes you already know both facts. My father's eyes are big and blue and sort of crazy looking, if you ask my mother, or at least unsettling, if you ask my sister. His eyes are unavoidably noticeable, at any rate, just like his bad jokes. I have my father's eyes, except mine are brown, not blue.

Let me tell you something about girls' underpants, in case you are unfamiliar. Perhaps boys' underpants work the same way, I wouldn't know. Underpants for little girls don't have elastic at the leg openings— instead they have a band of cotton, which is nice and soft until it gets baggy. Once your underpants have been washed enough times, the leg openings get to be the size of your head and no matter what you do, you will be picking underwear out of your butt every time you wear them.

My father thought my underwear difficulties were hysterical, and I have albums full of pictures of myself picking underwear out of my crack: in shorts, in jeans, at the beach, on a skiing trip. My dad was an amateur photographer with expensive cameras. He had his own darkroom when I was growing up. It wasn't like the only time my father took a picture of me I just happened to be picking at my bottom. Rather, it was his favorite subject matter or maybe he wanted to make a photojournalistic essay of it. He could have entitled it: *My Daughter Resolving Her Underwear Issues.*

The downside of his amusement over my underwear calamities is that I have very few decent pictures of myself as a child. We would spend every summer with our father and return to our mother's care with a scrapbook of our Alaskan adventures. Apparently, my adventures consisted mostly of battling my underpants. The pictures I do have are viewed under a haze of resentment and are not very satisfying. My mother didn't make us scrapbooks at all, so there is no proof that I was ever anything but a girl always pulling underwear out of her crack, with almost the same unsettling eyes as her father.

Memory Dissection: A Statue, My Father, and a Camera

The Victim

The bronze statue looked almost alive—a young girl, life-sized, or nearly. Her small breasts and slim hips placed her at the start of puberty, around twelve or thirteen—we were about the same age. Her mouth was open in a perfect oval.

I have looked extensively online, but I find no record of this statue anywhere. Perhaps the fact that she is untraceable, nameless, and lost to me makes her more poignant, like a commentary on young faceless women waiting to be victimized.

I realize that some will find my use of the word "victim" in conjunction with a statue hyperbolic.

The Incident

My father was attending a conference for the American Academy of Pediatrics in Washington, DC, and my brother and I joined him.

Dad liked photography and carried a camera bag everywhere he went, which he called his "purse." It contained his Olympus camera, wallet, sunglasses, stethoscope, a complete first-aid kit, including pre-threaded sterile needles for emergency stitches, and an empty can of Spam to use as a prop. He liked to pose his subjects.

We came across the statue in an outdoor garden, somewhere near the Smithsonian strip by the National Mall. There were no guards or docents to protect her, no security cameras or alarms, not even a "Do Not Touch" sign. As if she was asking for it.

My father pulled his camera from his bag, and he asked me to cup the statue's breasts and stick my tongue into her open mouth. I refused. He mocked my prudishness. I felt dirty, bad, vulnerable. I told myself that I was probably too sensitive, as he insisted, but still I refused.

A dozen years later my father took my stepmother to this same garden. He asked her to stick her tongue in the same statue girl's mouth. I know because I saw the photograph. "He asked me to do this, too," I told her. My stepmother said she felt wrong, dirty, and ashamed that she acquiesced, but she didn't know how to refuse my father. She, too, suspected that she was just being too sensitive. There is a line between appropriate and not, but that line undulates around my father.

An Interesting aside

After my mother and father divorced, my mother remarried a woman. After he and his next wife divorced, she also chose the companionship of women. The fact that two out of his six ex-wives are now lesbians wounds my father. I find this inexplicable. They did not leave him for women, they left him because of his infidelity. What came afterwards is not his concern. I don't know why it bothers him so much. Would he really prefer to think of them with other men?

After both of my divorces, my father asked if I were a lesbian, like my mother. When I said no, his relief was audible through the phone. A lesbian daughter would be too much for him to bear.

There is something here about women who don't need men, or who don't respect men's position of authority over women that is trying to come to the surface. Something about subservience and humiliation. Something about asking a woman to molest a statue, instead of asking us to hold the camera while he did it himself.

Fearless Girl

A bronze statue of a young defiant girl by Kristen Visbal was installed on the International Day of Women opposite the famous Wall Street Bull. A man in a business suit humped the statue and was caught on film, spurring public outrage and condemnation of rape culture.

THE TRUTH ABOUT UNRINGING PHONES

Some men, including my father, feel a stir around frozen, voiceless girls. Some men rub the bull's testicles for luck. It seems to be about what you can get away with. A statue, after all, has no feelings to protect, no ability to call for help, doesn't bruise and sheds no tears. Molesting a statue is not a crime. It just feels like one.

Fragments of Doubt

A few years ago my stepmother went out of town and left my father alone for a few days. Juli was responsible for picking him up for church. When she arrived, he answered the door stark naked.

"Is his dementia getting worse?" I asked her on the phone.

"No, it's just Dad being Dad," she said.

For her it was simple, but doubt licked at the edges of my mind—did he do it because he was free to be himself around the Lillibridge children, or because he somehow got off on exposing himself to his daughters?

Second Chances

When my father married Teresa, his sixth wife, she had two preschool aged boys, whom she called Duracell and Hemorrhoid. I no longer remember their given names, and it's better to leave them anonymous.

"Sharon [Juli's mother, his second wife] up in heaven sent me Teresa to be my wife and give me a second chance at being a father," Dad told me. Never mind that he was two wives past Sharon when she died.

Dad had left Sharon after the death of their eldest daughter, and she had never remarried and died of Diabetes when Juli was sixteen.

"After Dad and your mom broke up, my mom asked me if I thought she and Dad had any chance of getting back together," Juli told me. "I told her no, because I couldn't watch her go through that again."

When Sharon was in the hospital on life support, Dad was married to Margaret, wife #4. He flew down to see Sharon and Juli and told Sharon that she had always been the love of his life, and if she lived, he'd remarry her. Dad always loved the romance of the un-requited, the impossible, the inappropriate and unavailable.

"Your father loves the idea of being in love," my mother used to tell me after each of his divorces. "He loves to fall in love while he's married to someone else, feel that depth of despair, and ride the roller coaster into the next marriage. He doesn't actually love people so much as the romance of the situation."

Sharon believed him, and wanted to marry him again, I was told, but it was too late.

His marriage to Teresa (wife #6) lasted ten months, and after the divorce he never saw her children—his second chances at fatherhood—ever again.

But wait.

When Dad met Tricia, wife #7 and a widow, he told me how her husband in Heaven and Sharon (still in Heaven) got together and brought Dad and Tricia together so she could be his "one true love and second chance at being a father."

I still considered myself in need of fathering. I didn't consider my time as his child as past tense.

Tricia told me about how much she and Dad had in common as widows.

"Tricia, Dad was two wives beyond Sharon when she died. He was not a widower," I corrected.

"Well, it hurt him as if they were still married," she said.

Tricia did turn out to be the wife who stayed, and her children were indeed his second, third, fourth, and fifth chances at being a father. He taught them to ride bikes, went to their concerts and graduations. He did all the things with them he never did with me. Of course he loves them and is proud of them—compared to them, I'm a stranger, a weird left-over child who showed up a few weeks a year. They had to put up with his creepiness, his combination of strictness and neglect far more than I did. They have probably longer lists than I do of resentments against my father. Perhaps the best thing about my relationship with my father is that I did not live with him full-time.

I always assume their mother protected them from him, like she protected me from seeing him naked when she was around. I hope that when he sexualized everything—like writing his return address as "Limestone Circumcision" instead of "Limestone Circle" she crossed it out and got a new envelope. I assume so because if she didn't or couldn't, that means my waffling on whether his actions were abusive or just weird made her children vulnerable. I don't ask because I can't bear to know.

A Justifiable Unjustified Fear of Spiders

"Covert incest refers to a form of emotional abuse in which the relationship between a parent and a child is inappropriately sexualized without actual sexual contact." (Wikipedia)*
* Wikipedia is not considered a reliable source for scholarly articles.

For as long as I can remember, I have been afraid of spiders. Tricky things, they seem to be made not of legs, but hands. My fear is not based on a possible bite—a spider has bitten me only once that I can remember. I was five, and there was an old wooden boat in our backyard. My family and I lived in a rented house at the top of a hill, part of the payment my mother received for nannying the nine children that lived in the big house at the bottom of the hill while she was in grad school. This was the house Mom and Pat moved into together, the year my father moved to Alaska, and it was yellow. The boat belonged to the family in the big house, but was situated closer to ours, so we could play on it, too.

It was shaped like a tugboat, made out of wood with a small cabin you could go in and out of, and had a steering wheel that turned. There were knobs and dials that didn't work, so it was the steering wheel my brother and I fought over. He was older, so he won most of the time. The wood of the boat was splintery, dull brown, with no paint on the deck, but blue and red remnants on the exterior. The sides of the boat rose bowl-like to my waist and on the top rail there once was a yellow-brown striped spider, the size of a quarter. I don't know how it came to bite me, but I remember that it did, and I can clearly remember the red raised pinhead with white pus beneath. But that was the only time a spider bit me that I am aware of.

I'm not afraid of wasps, though I have been stung several times. Once, I ate an apple, high above the ground in a maple tree. A wasp found me, and all I could do was stay as still as I could, holding my breath, feeling my pulse so fast and hard it seemed I could hear it. The wasp landed on the knuckle of my index finger, and still I didn't move. Its proboscis sipped apple juice off my skin. Slowly I opened my fingers, and the apple dropped to the ground, the wasp following it.

The fear of spiders had to do with their ability to jump, and the feel of their hand-like feet scurrying down my legs, back, or arms. Small fluttering finger-legs running across my skin. The possibility of a spider caught in my hair. The idea that at night they could descend into my half-open slumbering mouth and I could swallow them and not even know it.

A spider in a corner cannot be trusted. It can descend at any moment, leap through the air and land on my knee, scurry up my thigh and I just know if I try to shoo it off it will run around behind me where I can't see it and the only way to get it off would be to strip down and jump in the shower. But what if there isn't a shower nearby? Once it was on me, its wiliness would make it impossible to catch, its finger-hand-feet running up and down my skin. It could end up anywhere, in any crevice.

My family went nude camping in the woods, so this was a legitimate fear. I often had no waistbands or elastic leg openings to protect me from a spider that chose to jump on me and run up my leg. I do not remember this ever happening, I had no justification for this feeling of creepiness, no history. Of course Mom and Pat and even Dad in Alaska all told me that I was being foolish. That did not make this skin-crawling feeling, this hot and cold flash of fear abate. I knew the look of a spider. I knew what it wanted. Lack of evidence had no bearing on the certainty of predation. Finger-legs I could not stop from running up and down my young flesh and into my crevices, particularly the one in front, the one I thought of as my pussy willow. Spiders were not relegated to the woods. They lived in our house on Cooper Road and my father's house in Alaska.

When we visited our father, my brother and I stayed alone in a cabin without electricity, my father and his wife in another cabin twenty feet south. My half-sister and stepsisters slept in yet another cabin equidistant to the north. I was six, my brother seven. The cabins and woods were filled with daddy long legs, not even true spiders, my father told me with his hard cold stare that said not to be ridiculous. My father would take off his shirt and pants on summer days and walk around camp in only bikini underwear and boots. On his back was a mole with long hairs that looked like a daddy long legs embedded in his flesh. Words running over my skin like spider feet. Eyes skimming my body like fingers. We slept alone, no lights, who knows how many daddy long legs and regular spiders lurking under our old metal camp beds. At least during the day, I had a chance to see them coming and run. During the day my older sister would guard me, but I knew my brother was as much prey as I was and was useless in the dark.

When I got married, my first husband was big and strong and tough. He was a biker, a hockey player, a person who lifted heavy objects for fun. He wasn't afraid of spiders. He would tear off their heads and shit down their throats to protect me. We lived in a 1950s tract home at the edge of the ghetto. Once I put on my jeans, fresh from the closet shelf, black jeans, size five, I was twenty years old, and something soft ran down my leg. I thought it was dog hair, but no, it was a millipede—a million-pede—four inches long and a zillion legs and it had been on my flesh and I didn't know if there were more and I didn't even know that it wasn't only spiders but other bugs that could startle me and crawl their tiny feet-hands all over my body. I screamed and stripped and jumped in the shower even though it made me late for work. And my husband laughed, of course, because he wasn't scared of anything at all, and wasn't I ridiculous? It was my tortoiseshell cat, Persephone, that hunted the big scary bugs in the house and ate them and kept me safe. This small ten-pound creature of mottled yellow gray and brown with an odd colored nose was the only one on my side.

My second husband was afraid of insects. He would not kill bugs for me, neither would he call the pizza place when the order was wrong. Neither of us ventured into the basement where the wolf spiders lived.

When I got divorced again, my children and I moved into a house that was nearly one hundred years old, with hardwood floors and built-in cabinets, and about a million spiders. I could not be afraid anymore. There was no one to protect me, and my ex-husband had kept the cat. So when my children and I moved into the old blue house that I loved so much, I knew it was up to me to make peace with the spiders.

I made a deal with them. Any spider smaller than a nickel would be allowed to stay, and I would agree not to be afraid. A spider the size of a nickel but smaller than a quarter that lived inside the house would be relocated to the outside, and I would let them live. Anything the size of a quarter or larger would have to be killed in any way possible. Only three times in five years did I have to eradicate a spider from my bedroom ceiling. Each time, my heart slamming into my ribs, my skin burned hot and cold tingling as I raised a shoe and killed it, terrified it would leap at the last minute, land on my arm and scurry under my clothes. But each time, I was my own heroine, a formidable foe, a victorious conqueror. Each time, after my heart quieted, I remained standing.

Multiple Choice

The shame comes from not objecting and not knowing (even now, as you sit in your chair in your living room at 47 years old) if you even had something to object to. You keep erasing your answers and choosing a different one.

    A. He didn't know better. His attachment disorder or other undiagnosed conditions meant that he really didn't know, and to complain, like you did in high school, was like kicking the dog who only wanted you to pet him behind the ears.

    B. He knew.

    C. He knew and you knew and you let it go on because you didn't want to risk his love. (Obviously there is something wrong with you for wanting his love.)

    D. It was nothing and you're too sensitive.

Where Are Daddy's Pants?

I can picture my Dad's favorite wool coats: one a red and black plaid, and the other blue-gray. I can picture his T-shirts, and how they ended right below his belly button. I can picture his striped bikini underwear and how they often split up the crack, but he wore them anyway. "It's from my mighty farts!" he liked to say.

I can clearly picture his blue-headed flaccid penis, his white legs and the bluish scar from when he was stabbed in the leg with a pencil in grammar school. He had a few moles with hairs growing out of them on his back. I know he wore black dress socks. He was partial to loafers for work or hiking boots. He called sneakers "tenny-runners" and I think he wore New Balance. But for the life of me, I can't remember what kind of pants my father wore.

Look, he must have worn pants on the boat, in the woods, while driving the car. He used to wear three-piece suits to work and then gray dress pants with pastel shirts with matching ties and suspenders (thanks, sis, for encouraging that fashion disaster). But after hours, when he got home did he wear jeans? Corduroys? Khakis?

Floating on a River of Smoke

The first place Dad lived when he moved to Alaska was a condo he called the Hampton House, named for the road it was built on. It was new 1970s construction. He told me that condos were the most efficient housing in Alaska because of shared heat in the cold. We were supposed to think of the Hampton House as our "Alaska home," though we didn't have our own rooms, or toys, or books there. How could it be home without even a bed to sleep in?

Dad and Margaret converted the living room into their bedroom, and they slept on a king-sized futon they rolled up every morning. There was no couch—only a pile of floor pillows Margaret sewed, and two orange director's chairs that faced the curtainless large windows that looked out on Baxter Bog and the mountains beyond. Margaret hung cut crystals from the windowsills to dance in the sunlight. I liked to run my hand through the rainbow they projected onto the brown carpeting.

Dad had a big stereo system he kept on a long wooden board, which sat on two concrete blocks, and he had a strobe light. There was a small TV and later a VCR in the corner, and Matt and I sat on the floor to watch it while they were at work—mainly Star Wars, but occasionally porn the adults (accidentally?) left behind. There was a large walk-in closet off the living room where Dad and Margaret kept their clothes.

The first floor of the condo had two small bedrooms and a full bath off a dark hallway. That was where all the kids slept. Every summer I had the same nightmare that I couldn't explain: floating faces, a river of smoke.

The second floor held the kitchen, half-bath, and the living room/bedroom. It was the only house I'd ever been in with a second-floor kitchen. It had a trash compactor, which I had never seen before, and a few years later, a microwave. I thought every house in Alaska had a trash compactor because Dad said they couldn't dig big garbage pits because of the frozen ground. I didn't yet know about the piles of trash outside the Native villages. He didn't have a basement because you couldn't dig below the frost line. Under the house was an unfinished crawl space—rocky dirt covered with plastic sheeting. We had to pull the trap door up and jump down into the underbelly of the house to retrieve the camping gear, and since I was smallest, I was always asked to help. I was terrified of getting closed in down there, of darkness and spiders and locked hatches, but I also kind of loved being the right size to fit underneath the ceiling without ducking much. I wanted more than anything to be short, like Juli.

Once Dad asked me to answer the door while he read the newspaper naked in the living room. Dad was often naked, so I was surprised that he was angry when I let the stranger in. Dad whispered he wasn't "that kind of friend" to invite in without clothing. But I didn't know any of Dad's friends, so how was I supposed to sort out clothed friends from naked friends?

The man was younger than dad with big curly hair and a mustache. Like a cross between Bob Ross and Barney Miller. He didn't seem to mind that Dad was buck naked, crouched over the newspaper on the floor. He insisted there was no reason for Dad to get dressed, though Dad grabbed a robe and glowered at me.

My father was proud of his body, walking tall with his head back and perfect posture, even when naked. He was, I got the impression, proud of his penis—the way he talked about it and made sure we noticed it. He liked to wear little colored bikini underwear without a fly that always split up the back, and he liked to dance and shake his hips wearing nothing but bikinis—not for laughs, but in a show-off-y, "look at me, I'm a great dancer" type of way.

I was young enough back then to take a bath with my father, or a shower with his wife. They used Flex shampoo, the same brand as my mother. There was a loofah that scratched, soap that burned between my legs. Margaret said I could just wash with water.

I pulled up the Hampton House on Zillow, and even with new carpeting the remnants of nightmares linger in the walls of the floorplan. The bathroom. The back bedroom. The living room. I close my computer so I don't have to remember. I don't have many memories of what happened there, only terror and deep stomach clenching dread as vivid as when I was six years old.

Fragments on Yearning: Texts

Juli: I'll call Dad every night and you can call him every morning.

Me: Juli, I don't want a relationship with Dad.

Juli: He's all alone, sis.

Me: Did you ask Matt? Matt still has warm feelings for him.

Scrapbook:
Visit to Alaska February 12-28, 1982 (Second Grade)

Daddy took my picture with the 1982 Fur Rendezvous Queen. She is so beautiful, and I'm wearing my winter coat from the boy's section in the discount section. It's pink, but the color of insulation in the attic, not pretty pink, and Mommy swears no one will know it's a boy's coat, but I know, and besides it's dirty and my hat is yellow and they don't match.

Daddy knows one of the hot air balloon guys, and we get to go right up close, but not into the basket. We watch them rise into the cold, thin air.

We stand on the roof of some building to watch the grand prix, and one car flipped over right below us and it's just like in a movie only real and right here.

Matt got to race Dad's friend's dog, Kevak, who is half-malamute half-husky and super fluffy. He came in 9th. Daddy said I'll get to race next year.

Matt and I got into a fight and he was chasing me and when I ran out of the bedroom, I slammed the door behind me so he couldn't catch me, but I slammed his finger in the door and Dad gave him two stitches and a finger splint. Dad put the needle and suture in our scrapbook along with a polaroid of Matt, who is smiling the happiest smile I've ever seen.

We went to the blanket toss and the model train exhibit. Dad's dog, Nuni, ran away in the park because he lets her run off the leash. Someone thought they found her, but it was not the same dog. Dad called the new dog Xerox, but we couldn't keep her.

The best part of Fur Rondy is the indoor fair, and I bought a furry pink pet ice worm (it's really just fabric with googly eyes, but if you pet it a certain way it moves like it's real.) There was a 'panning for gold' booth and I spent all the rest of my money there, swirling the silt in my pan, finding a handful of dark burgundy garnets, and they are the exact color of blood and probably worth $60 the guy at the booth said, if I polished them up.

After Fur Rondy was over we went to Loon Landing, which is a four-hour drive. On the way we picked up a hitchhiker names Spook. She said she talked in her sleep so her brothers gave her that name. She had long blond hair in two braids, and she carried everything she owned in a backpack. I sat in the back of the van on the orange shag carpet. When we got to the campground it was ten degrees below zero, but we lit a fire in the wood stove and the thermometer went up to 110. It was like a sauna in there. We use oil lamps for light since there is no electricity here. We have to do our homework because we're missing school. Also, I lost a tooth.

We skied across Lake Louise to the Lake Louise Lodge which is a bar, so kids can't sit on the tall stools, only at the tables. Dad won't give us money for pool so Matt and I hit around the cue ball and rubbed the blue chalk on the ends of our noses. On the way back across the lake I was skiing on one foot because my ski fell off. The next day we sledded down the hill and used our sleds to lug firewood back to the cabins. Another day we went ice fishing.

I drew a picture of myself and Matt wrote on it, "I am a idit. I am a brat. I stink. P.S. I hate me." I tried to erase it but it didn't work so I put a line through it. Dad put the drawing in the scrapbook anyway, I don't know why.

When we went back to Anchorage we got stuck in a snowbank and had to get the shovels and dig out the van which took 18 minutes. We went to Cora's gas station to call Margaret but the line was busy. On the way home we played "I Spy" and sang songs and ate granola bars, bologna, and carrots.

We drove down to Seward for Dad to do a clinic. It was really cold and I wore my orange ski hat that covers my face. Dad made us sit on a giant anchor and took our pictures. I hate being cold.

We had a birthday party for Matt since his birthday is March 1. Dad's nurse's kids came and some other kids Dad knows who live nearby. We had a paper airplane contest, a headstand contest, and a balloon sword fight. I'm really bad at making paper airplanes.

Rejections

When I was in fourth grade my father came to visit me and Matt in Rochester, where we lived with our mother and her wife, Pat. It was the first time he had ever come to see us, instead of us flying to see him. Dad stayed at his friends' house—a Jewish couple who lived one block up and three streets over from us. My brother and I visited with the wife, Sylvia, every Thursday. Sometimes she took us to Friendly's Restaurant and let us order anything we wanted—once my brother ate four sundaes in one sitting. Other times we went to her house and looked at the few games her grown sons had left behind. We played Sorry because we didn't know how to play Backgammon. Sylvia gave us snacks in her small kitchen. There was a wall hanging of the Hebrew alphabet next to the Formica table and a wall-mounted telephone they didn't answer on the Sabbath.

When it was our birthdays, Sylvia took my brother or me to the toy store and let us pick out anything we wanted, and she said that Dad would mail her a check. I wonder now if he ever did, or if she even asked him to.

It was common knowledge that Sylvia was in love with my father. Her husband, Bernie, didn't seem to mind. I wasn't sure if they all slept in the same bed when my father stayed with them—it seemed most logical to my nine-year-old self, who had already witnessed him having such arrangements with other adults in Alaska, like Wanda with the gold fingernails, who stayed in the one-room cabin with Dad and his wife Margaret.

Dad asked to come to school with us—one day with me, one day with my brother. I was shocked that the teacher agreed, and although I worried a bit about the social ramifications I was too young to be really appalled. My dad was my favorite person in the whole world—I was sure my friends would think the same. Dad sat next to me in a little desk. I tried to cheat on my Social Studies test and passed him a note asking him an answer I didn't know.

"Ronald Regan," he wrote back. I did the patented daughter eyeroll. Regan was the current president, and we were studying Colonialism.

"If you don't know the answer, be funny," he told me. The problem was, I didn't think his answer was funny enough to submit to my teacher. She was my favorite teacher of all time—the only teacher I had actually liked since kindergarten. On the first day of school, she told our class that we were, "the cream of the fourth grade crop." That was the first time I knew I was smart. My best friend was not in the same class, ergo, she was not the cream of the crop. I never told her, but I never forgot it. The next year we were in the same class again, so had she gotten smarter or had I gotten stupider. I worried that it was the latter.

When Dad came to visit that week in fourth grade, I was struggling to learn my times tables. I tried; I really did. I even stayed after school for an hour and cleaned out Dwayne's desk because he promised to teach me to multiply in exchange—we were learning about bartering—but all he did was give me an index card with the table printed on it that he'd gotten somewhere. My teacher reprimanded him for his lack of effort, but it still didn't teach me the math. My father sat at the picnic table in the backyard of my mother's house and went over them with me. He got up and did a knobby elbows and knees sort of dance around the yard chanting the six tables, "six times eight is forty-eight." Every test I ever took, every calculation I ever did for the rest of my life involving that equation I hear my father's voice in my head. It is the only reason I passed math that year.

We carved pumpkins, so it must have been October. Daddy asked us what we wanted to create. I don't remember what I said, but we did mine first and I gave explicit and unimaginative instructions. Dad did exactly as I asked him to do. When it was my brother's turn, Dad attached chunks of pumpkin to straws and make alien antennae, then Dad used toothpicks to make sticky-outie ears on his own pumpkin. I wished I hadn't been in such a rush to go first, hadn't been so strong-willed in what I thought I wanted. Perhaps that was when I learned it was better to hang back a little, not to trust my own opinion so much. This was both the right lesson and the one wrong one.

Dad went back to Alaska and the rest of the school year was less bright. When he was with us, my brother and I were shiny, smart, beautiful, interesting. When he left, it was months of radio silence—a few letters, the rare phone call. The world was darker and bleaker—our town was one of the most overcast in the nation.

I'm sure he saw our vacations as quality time, a way to fill our emotional and memory reserves. I know he thought it was just as good as living in the same state.

When Matt was nineteen and I was eighteen, my brother's ex-girlfriend got pregnant. She gave my brother the choice to be involved or not, but he couldn't flow in and out of this new child's life. He had to commit one way or the other. My brother knew he couldn't be the father he wanted to be at that time, so he chose to relinquish his rights. My brother said then that he would have been better off had Dad died when we were children than having the sporadic spotlight of his affection.

I don't think my brother was wrong. I was always in a state of longing, of feeling unwanted, of waiting for a phone to ring or for him to surprise me with an unexpected appearance at a school concert *a la* Lifetime Movie.

Once when I was around nine or ten Dad called and I answered the phone. It was my brother's birthday. "Daddy!" I yelled. Joy surged in my voice, my being. He called. He called and I answered and surrounded by long-distance static was my Daddy's voice.

"Let me talk to Matt," he said.

"But can't I talk to you, too?" I asked.

"It's not your birthday," he said.

Wish Night

The Unitarian church ran a summer camp in the Adirondack mountains, a few hours from our home in upstate New York. My brother and I went for several summers in high school. One night was designated, "wish night" where every camper could wish for anything in the world they wanted, and another camper would be assigned to fulfill their wish. Anything.

I helped arrange for Godzilla and King Kong to dance in a mosh pit. Someone else asked simply for a cool "hair thing." I asked for my father to love me as much as he loved my brother.

I knew it was a big ask. I knew it was unreasonable and improbable, but I pictured them calling my father in Alaska, him calling in or sending a telegraph…OK, let's be honest, I might have envisioned a helicopter depositing my father on the soccer field.

Instead, Doug, a Counselor in Training who went on to become a minister, called me to the stage and read my wish aloud. I started to cry as soon as I heard my name. Doug told me that he could never fulfill my wish, but that I had my brother, my friends, and Doug himself who would step in and take my father's place in my life. He hugged me and I cried in front of everyone until I didn't need to cry any more.

Labels Attached to my Father

Self-claimed:

    A. Attachment disorder

    B. Sex addict

    C. Alcoholic (sober since 1986)

Attributed by others:

    1. Asperger's/Autism Spectrum Disorder
    2. Narcissistic Personality Disorder
    3. Pervert

What combination justifies my blame? What combination lets me walk away guilt-free?

What combination means what the fuck is wrong with me for even trying to measure my own guilt in abandoning him?

Can it all be explained as the quintessential God complex of the American doctor, the inevitable result of a patriarchal white supremacist society which allows certain men to act as demagogues and reinforces that the rules don't apply to them?

My sister just calls it "being a Lillibridge" and perhaps there is something polluted in our blood, something inherited, a double-twisted segment of our DNA.

There is a Facebook group dedicated to the Lillibridge family history. A Lillibridge I have never met posted this article from The Sioux City Journal, Sioux City, Iowa, Wed, Apr 28, 1897 · Page 5. My first cousin says the men in question are my great-uncles.

ALIENATION OF AFFECTIONS
John W. Lillibridge, of Kossuth County, Sues His Brother on This Charge.
SAYS HIS HOME WAS BROKEN UP
His Wife, He Alleges, Was Seduced by His Brother, of Whom He Seeks Damages in the Sum of $10,000—Adjourned Session of District Court Today.

My biggest fear is that I have inherited something twisted from my father. As I type my heartrate climbs. What does it mean to be a Lillibridge, descendant of generations of Lillibridges known for sexual indiscretion?

- My father—obviously.

  - His father—known philanderer. Once my grandmother threw all three kids in the car and drove from Olympia, Washington to the air base in California where he was stationed in order to catch him in the act. My father said the car was hot and the trip was long.

My father says the only happy relationship he witnessed as a child was between his father and his mistress—he used to eat dinner with them some nights.

  - And now these great-uncles. Damages for loss of affection—did he want the $10,000 as moral retribution, or to pay for consortium elsewhere? I can give him the benefit of the doubt and say it is for childcare—they had two daughters in five years. If I trace my lineage to this couple, did I inherit more genetic material from the philandering brother or the runaway wife?

Complicity

My father liked to take us to work with him—it was his dream to have at least one child follow him into medicine, though none of us were interested.

When I was a teenager he gave me a hospital coat and told the parents I was a medical student, and when I objected to the deception he told me, "you could be, you don't know what you want to major in yet." He dragged me into routine exams of kids only a few years younger than I was, their privacy of no concern to him. The parents always fawned over him, and praised me for following him into the family business. I didn't like being complicit in his story.

Complicit has a soft tone when spoken, compared to the harshness of *conniving* or the knife edge of *deceit*. Writers talk about *reader complicity* as if there was no crime involved, as if it meant only being part of a secret or solving a mystery, but that's not how the word is intended. *Complicit* rests on an underlying shadow.

I did not ever think of the privacy I invaded as I peered over his shoulder. I didn't like the lie because it aligned me too closely with my father, not because I thought it was unfair to the patient. Perhaps I had already assimilated to the medical view: people are interesting specimens, and the privacy of children is the purview of the parent to give away with the scrawl of a pen or a nod of the head. "Yes, she can observe my child's pain."

No one ever objected to my presence. Is it fair to judge the pre-HIPAA hospital with post-HIPAA standards? After all, during this time period, it was common practice for medical students to perform their first pelvic exams on anesthetized women without any consent at all. A doctor's kid looking over someone's shoulder seems almost innocent in comparison.

Procedures I observed at my father's elbow:
- Colonoscopy of a ten-year-old
- Several endoscopes
- An esophageal stretching

As a young child, I spent hours waiting on hard plastic chairs in hospital hallways or pushing tasteless food around my plate in the hospital cafeteria. Dad would pull me into an exam room now and then to see a particular case, like a toddler who screamed uncontrollably when they removed his clothes and held him face down on the stainless-steel table. "He knows that when he comes to the hospital, it hurts," my father explained, "but if we don't fix it, he'll die."

Being both the bringer of life and pain seems the best description I can think of for my father, and also there is something in there about showing me bodies like curiosities.

But for me, being present in the room was bearing witness. The children's screams remain trapped in my cochlea, even if the patients themselves have forgotten. I was never good at detachment. Observing strengthened my resolve never to go into medicine.

I had never seen Dad make a house call. People came to him, people waited for him, whether for a medical procedure or a dinner party. Many times I'd see him answer a page and advise a patient to proceed to the emergency room immediately, then leisurely finish eating dinner. "They'll wait" was his philosophy. So when Dad said we were going to a patient's house when I was around eight years old it was downright weird. My brother did not come with us. I'm unsure where Matt was that day and if he refused to come, or just wasn't around, but I am clear that I had no choice, and that I was the only child present.

Dad and I pulled up to a house overflowing with people. The front door was open and Black people of all ages cascaded down the porch and pooled in groups on the lawn. It seemed to be a very large family party. I was an anxious, shy kid—not quiet, I was a nervous talker—but scared of gatherings where I didn't know anyone, and there were twenty or more people here, so I asked to wait in the car. Dad refused. He wanted me with him, though he told me nothing as to why.

I wasn't allowed to be shy, and I wasn't allowed to refuse Dad, so I closed the door of his Subaru station wagon and followed him inside, as close to his elbow as I could manage. The kids on the lawn looked at me and Dad and glanced away, murmuring to themselves. It was obvious that we were intruders, and the whiteness of our skin made it even clearer.

The river of people parted in front of us as we pushed through the hall into the living room, where a large woman sat on the couch, wailing and clutching her baby to her chest. I had never heard an adult sob so loudly.

Dad whispered to me that the baby was dead, and she refused to give her child's body to the medical personnel who had come to retrieve it.

Dad spoke quietly and gently to the mother. "It's time," he said, and she handed over her deceased child to the medical attendants without words, sobbing louder. The women in the room surrounded her like water rushing in to fill the empty space. I could no longer see her over the heads of the adults, though the sound of her grief followed us out. Dad and I walked quickly down the hallway, got in the car and left. He didn't explain if the baby had been his patient or if he was covering for another doctor that day, nor did he tell me how the baby had died. As with many things, Dad's explanation was incomplete, and I knew better than to ask.

Although the grieving mother's body was not splayed open on an exam table, she was naked and vulnerable in a deeper way than any other time I was forced to witness. I was not a willing intruder, but the end result is that I intruded. He had a reason to be there. I did not. He made me complicit.

Would he have dragged me along if the family were white?

Was this something about being liberal and meant to show me how colorblind he was?

Or was his motivation completely different—was bringing his daughter a way to remind the mother that he was a father, and therefore understood her pain?

Was it as simple as he didn't want to leave me in the car alone in that particular neighborhood—wherever it was?

Perhaps, he wanted to show me how revered he was yet again, how being a doctor was more than stethoscopes around your neck and patients waiting in hospital exam rooms.

Or maybe in the end, he only wanted to underscore the inconvenience of the house call, and I was to stand as a silent reprimand of the interruption to his life.

Decades later, I remembered that mother when I held my own fragile, tiny babies. I could understand her need to hold on to them just a little bit longer, her unending grief. I want to tell her I'm sorry I was a spectator to her mourning, that I held her grief close as I nursed my own newborn child, praying for the angel of death to pass me over.

Bean Kitchen

When I was twenty-three I worked for a life insurance and mutual fund company. I put together a retirement plan for my father. Dad and Tricia were still working full-time, and he had a retirement fund and would receive a decent amount of social security. His wife had a pension. It sounded good but I knew how much more he needed to keep up his extravagant lifestyle. Dad's retirement account only contained employer contributions, he had never saved a dime of his own. He had no savings account, and lived paycheck to paycheck, though his income was larger than most people would ever make—myself included.

We talked about how much he needed to save while he was still working and Dad pulled me to his chest. His body shuddered as he loudly sobbed, saying that he never wanted to end up "old and eating at the bean kitchen."

I promised that I would keep him out of the bean kitchen.

I assured him he could take care of himself if only he exercised a little restraint now, while he still could. Instead, he went on yearly vacations to Europe with the Anchorage Concert Chorus, to Mexico with Tricia and her kids. Russia, New Zealand, Prague. He spent $100,000 on plans for a boat that he couldn't afford to build. He emptied his retirement account to build a custom home he designed himself. And then there were the presents Tricia loved to buy her children.

By the time he ran out of money, I had run out of sympathy.

Oh, Christmas Tree

I spent one Christmas Day with my father. I was ten and in the fifth grade.

My Mom and Pat didn't have much extra money, and what they had went into savings for college. We didn't have Jordache jeans or rabbit fur jackets like the other kids at school, and we couldn't buy hot lunch in the cafeteria very often. But every year they pulled off the best Christmas ever.

Christmas Eve, we got to stay up late for the 11:00 PM service. I stood next to my soft huggable mother, listening to her low voice sing *Silent Night* as they turned off the overhead lights, so the sanctuary was lit only by the candles we each held in our hands. Christmas morning, Matt and I woke to find our parents' digital clock at the top of the stairs and a piece of tinsel garland roping off the hallway. This was always the same and always part of the magic.

My brother and I would whisper and dream of what was downstairs and it was the one day when we never fought and I was always grateful to have a brother. 8:30 AM meant we got to wake Mom and Pat and race downstairs for presents and more presents, and stockings stuffed with candy, and Mom home all day long and no one fighting. We got to eat ourselves sick on chocolate before breakfast. Mom didn't even insist on making coffee until after the presents were all opened—at least not until we were older. We didn't ever get everything on our lists, but we always got the top few things. As a parent, I understand now how much a Lego set or Barbie doll can cost, and it's a lot more than I ever imagined. We spent the run-up to Christmas—the catalog season—circling toys and dreaming, and Mom and Pat took us to the mall to buy our gifts for each other, and we weren't expected to save our allowance for that, either, though we did have a budget we had to stay inside of.

Christmas was hands-down my favorite day of the year, and offering it to Dad was the biggest gesture I could make: *here is everything I love best about my family, and I will give it up for you.*

I thought maybe it would make him love me best, choose me.

Matt stayed home with Mom and Pat. We had two trips to Alaska every year: a joint trip in the summer, and a week alone with Dad every winter. I chose Christmas for my alone week.

Dad was married to Jan then, and at that time they lived in two apartment buildings next to each other. Each building had four units, two upstairs, two down. I stayed in the lower-level one-bedroom Dad owned, and he and Jan lived in a two-bedroom on the second floor of the building next door, which she owned. That is to say, there wasn't room for Matt and me in their lives.

I arrived in town a few days before Christmas. Dad went to work and Jan and I cooked all day for a party they were having. She made things I'd never heard of, like divinity candy, and other things I'd heard of but never eaten, like lamb. The smell of the lamb made me sick to my stomach, and after a small bite I was allowed not to eat more. This was a rarity at my father's house—a Christmas miracle. It might have been different if there hadn't been a party—I had spent many a summer night staring down a piece of liver alone in the kitchen, not allowed to leave my chair until it was gone. Maybe they just didn't want me to fuss in front of their friends.

They had a bunch of people over I didn't know and we set out the food in a large buffet. I remember that day as neutral—bland, unmemorable. But that was OK because everything was about waiting for Christmas, and a child's job is to wait patiently through all the boring stuff and then you wake up on December twenty-fifth and it is magic and the culmination of every childhood wish. Besides, they didn't make me eat lamb.

Christmas Eve Dad gave Jan and me typed up copies of *The Best Christmas Pageant Ever* and we took turns reading it instead of going to church. It is still one of my favorite Christmas books.

Dad never got a Christmas tree until he married Tricia when I was nineteen. The most he ever did was decorate a branch with one string of lights and a garland, and not a big branch, but a dead, leafless one about two-feet tall he had stuck in a pot.

"There are too few tall trees in Alaska, it would be a crime to cut one down just to decorate a house with it," he explained. Anchorage was below the tree line, but not by much, and the evergreens were stunted, most not significantly more than five feet tall, and spindly. They looked like the kind of tree that if you decorated it, you'd feel sorry for both yourself and it.

We celebrated Christmas morning without a tree or stockings, sitting on the floor of Dad's apartment, next to a cold stone fireplace. At home we always had a fire on Christmas if we wanted one, and Jiffy Pop popcorn in the round tin cooked in the fireplace. I'm not sure Dad's fireplace even worked. There was no artwork on the walls. We sat on the floor because there was no sofa. All of that was upstairs in Jan's apartment, which was chock-full of cushy pillows and knickknacks.

Dad and Jan bought each other thick, white bathrobes, and matching shearling jackets. I'd seen them both in the Air Mall catalogs—my idea of the ultimate in luxury. I opened a present—a book, or socks. Something nice but not a toy or a new outfit.

And I sat there.

They had more gifts for each other, little thoughtful things, but nothing else for me.

"Your plane ticket cost over a thousand dollars," Jan said. "Christmas is the most expensive time to fly." She was the same wife who cut off Juli's child support when she was nineteen.

THE TRUTH ABOUT UNRINGING PHONES

I didn't cry or mope or anything. I recognized I'd chosen poorly. And the ticket was expensive, and they weren't kid people and didn't have room in their lives for me.

I mean to say that I was disappointed but not upset—I knew that I would still have Christmas back home with Mom and Pat in a few days. I just knew never to spend Christmas with Dad ever again, and I didn't, even the year I lived with him.

Choosing Dad

There were so many things wrong that year. Mom had emerged from eye surgery with partial paralysis in her arms. The doctors ran test after test but they didn't know what happened. Matt and I had to go buy groceries and wheel them a half a mile home with the old lady folding cart. I had to stay home that summer and help mom with eating, dressing, answering the phone. Mom didn't ask for much, but Pat used her "you better or else" voice which stripped the love from my actions and turned them into an obligation.

The boys barked at me at school because I was an ugly dog. Ruff-ruff and bow-wow and arrarararrar. Some people still called me Lara the Lezzie, in honor of my moms. We couldn't afford cool clothes and I was too smart, anyway. I wanted to go someplace where I could remake myself into someone new. I wanted to be beautiful. But more than that, I wanted to be loved by a boy. Desperately. So after I met a boy in Alaska, I asked Dad if I could move in with him, just a mile away from my new love. It didn't matter that the boy didn't love me.

I got to be the child who chose Dad. I got to be special, treasured even. Dad wrote me love letters (which I pretended weren't creepy) eerily similar to the ones he wrote his girlfriend Rose, who was relocating to Alaska from Texas to be the youth minister at his Methodist church. Dad hoped his divorce would go through by the time she got there, and that his current wife, Jan, whom he'd married in that same church, would be completely out of the picture. Dad shared Rose's letters with me and she called me, "Baby Girl," on the phone, sounding as excited to be my stepmother as she was to be dad's fiancé.

Rose arrived in Anchorage a few weeks before I did. My plane landed around 6:00PM. My father brought me to his apartment, fed me dinner, then left to stay at Rose's house. There was no TV, no radio, and her house didn't have a phone installed, since she'd moved in a few days prior. The Disney bluebirds flew away and I was just a girl alone in an apartment with a suitcase of clothes and a bag of Starburst candies.

Dad came back the next morning to take me to my new school. He brought me toast with peanut butter in bed, and didn't leave the room when I got dressed —watching me strip from his seat on my mattress. I wore my best denim high-top shoes, acid-washed jeans and jean jacket. At least at East Anchorage High they wouldn't know everything that shamed me. Maybe I could be popular, pretty, cool. Maybe the bluebirds would come back.

Fragment of a Song

My mother and father rewrote "The Sloop John B" when they went on vacation to Alaska and I was still in diapers. Dad sang me the song every summer.

> *We came with the Lara B.*
> *Matty, Daddy, and me.*
> *Around Anchorage town, we did roam.*
> *Drinking our juice,*
> *And looking for moose.*
> *Before the break-up, I want to go home.*

Once, I was loved.

I wonder who my father would have been to me if he and my mom stayed married, or if he had stayed in town, or if he had married someone who saw his biological children as having as much value as her own offspring.

But maybe seeing my father more would have been worse, not better. Maybe the only thing that saved me after all was the distance between us.

The Blue Hour

In winter, the Anchorage sun shines through the deep snow on the mountains, and the city is colored blue—lapis shadows, azure snow—everything is drenched in tones of the night sky or the deepest ocean until the sun rises high enough for the light to reach us unfiltered, ordinary once more. That isn't actually the true scientific explanation for the bluing, but it was the one my father gave me as an invitation into the magic of Alaskan winter. Revising memory to conform with facts erodes the feeling of wonder. Let it be sun and snow and latitude. Let me hold the memory of the glint of my father's ice-blue eyes and his smiled-crinkled face as he showed me the otherworldliness peculiar to his hometown.

That first hour feels like a blending of story and reality, a hint of places where magic could live, and as I watched, moose taller than a person walked slowly down the silent street. The snow was so cold it squeaked beneath the twist of my boot heel. There was no wind in the valley—never wind in the valley—and the snow fell soft and dreamlike unbuffeted, coming to rest on my Aquanet-shellacked hair like glitter. "Don't touch it," my father said. "Just let it dry, and your hair will be fine."

And it was.

But I was not fine in the land of forget-me-nots and fireweed, of never being warm enough and a sun that never set in the summer and only rose for a few hours in the winter. When I had detention, I went to school in the dark and returned home in the dark, the blue hour just a memory of when Anchorage was my vacation town, not my home. Instead, I looked out the window at snow-covered roads topped with a layer of sand because it was too cold for salt to be effective. The sun was always more white than yellow, colder and less friendly than the one back home. And yes, I saw the northern lights, and more than once, but I didn't know that once I left Alaska I'd be unable to see them in the same way again—the lower latitude robbed the bands of their color, and when I tried to explain how they really looked my words didn't sound real even to my own ears. I mean to say that I didn't know to cherish them.

Alaska was magic and untamed wilderness but also drugs and shoplifting and failing out of school. Anchorage's Spenard Road loomed like an alternate ending of my story—a place where in the 1980s Native girls disappeared only to be found dead with marks of torture on their young bodies—girls I resembled with my long dark hair, though I wasn't Native. Alaska's winter was the place where I couldn't raise myself out of the shadows to be my better self, but I meant to, and one day, I swore I'd come back after college and make myself and Alaska everything we both were capable of being, if only we had a bit more luck and if only the blue hour lasted just a little bit longer.

THE TRUTH ABOUT UNRINGING PHONES

And of course I never went back, despite my promise to the city. It was too far, too cold. It was, in the end, not my home though it cradled me nine months. At the end, I left it behind to live in the real world, meaning the lower forty-eight. The only other place that called to me in the same way as Alaska was Key West, the diagonal opposite end of the country, and though I loved that place, too, it was always as its stepchild, a slight distance between me and the people born there, notwithstanding the history I was building. I was born in the middle of the country and that's where I fit, where life will always feel real to me, even though it has no magic and no hour of blue but only overcast skies. The edges were someplace I tried on and longed to keep but somehow, the cost was always too high.

Field Notes on Damage

While we are all familiar with the oyster's pearl, all mollusks can produce calcareous concentrations when a microscopic irritant is introduced to its interior, even the escargot snail.

I didn't want to be a snail, but I knew I was one. I wore Lee jeans in a sea of Jordache. My indelicate, knobby wrists invariably stuck out two inches below my shirt cuffs. I had glasses *and* braces, and the only dimple I had was in the underside of my chin. I walked with my weight too far back in my heels, and I was gangly and uncoordinated—last picked in gym class. I knew too many answers in class, still fought with the boys on the playground, and detested carrying a purse. No amount of blue eyeshadow would make me an oyster, but that didn't stop me from layering it on, lash-line to eyebrow.

Like the escargot, however, males of my species were starting to see me as something worth eating. I had developed early.

Most gemologists agree that only the iridescent product that contains translucence has value.

THE TRUTH ABOUT UNRINGING PHONES

I was determined to be pretty. Peroxide turned my dark brown hair rust colored—it was too dark to bleach blond, but that was still an improvement. I spent hours curling and spraying my mullet into place. I melted the tip of my black eyeliner to make the line darker. I stopped wearing my glasses. I spent my babysitting money on a denim miniskirt, size three. I wished I were size zero. I tried my hardest not to eat, but my appetite betrayed me.

Kris was one of the few kids I knew in Alaska—his mother worked for my father, and we went to the same church. He was pimply, slightly chubby, and I thought his nose was weird. But he was something I wasn't—cool. Or so he told me, and so I believed. He had a car, gelled hair, a Forenza T-shirt and a west-coast accent. He kissed me. How could I not fall for him?

Mussels produce freshwater pearls. All freshwater pearls commercially available today are cultured.

I moved to Alaska, where I thought I could slip out from under the labels of nerd and geek, where no one would know boys barked at me in the cafeteria and girls made fun of my perfect elocution: *say twunny*, the four-foot tall bully said, riling the locker room full of half-naked girls into laughter at the crisp "ts" in the word when I repeated it: twenty. I wanted to be someone new.

I thought every woman in fashion magazines was a natural beauty, and no matter how hard I tried, I came up short. But I also knew I had great breasts. Everyone said so. Kris did not want to be my boyfriend, but he did want to touch me in the dark. Of course I let him. Maybe if I let him touch me enough he'd realize I was worth seeing in the light. Or maybe he'd at least keep coming around to visit. He was my first everything. All of it hurt. None of it was enough to make him want to be my boyfriend.

"You're a good girl. Find a guy who loves you," he said after he took my virginity, "and who has a bigger dick."

Sex wasn't enough to keep him coming over, but my best friend was. She was fragile, cute, stylish, and sassy. He asked her to go to the winter dance with him. He promised to find me a date, but the other kid never showed, and so I went to the dance with the two of them, since Suzy wanted me to, and I already had a dress. A dress that she later told me was completely wrong, though she'd helped me pick it out. But I already knew I was completely wrong, no matter how hard I tried.

In freshwater mollusks, merely opening the shell and cutting the mantle is enough to culture a pearl. No further irritant needs to be inserted.

I buried my face into my pillow and wailed when he kissed Suzy in my living room. I was afraid I'd never stop crying, this ache in my chest would tear me apart.

It was a one-bedroom apartment. My father converted the dining room into a bedroom for himself, though he mostly slept at his girlfriend's house down the street. He kept his dresser in my bedroom—used for storage, not clothes. And in the top drawer was his collection of pocketknives. He'd shown them to me, asked if any of my friends might be tempted to steal them. Told me they were sharp enough to slice a hair—so sharp they could cut me before I felt it. That sounded like exactly what I needed. I ran the blade across my ankle. A red line appeared. A droplet of blood ran down to the floor. The carpet was dark brown. I didn't bother wiping it up.

Rarely is the pearl started by a grain of sand in nature, regardless of common lore.

I knew slicing my wrists was overly dramatic. I knew that I would never be able to cut deeply enough to get the job done. And my mother—I couldn't do that to my mother, even though she was over 4,000 miles away.

These layers of calcium carbonate are formed as part of the mollusks immune system to protect the mollusk from parasites, damage, or an intrusion of organic material.

The physical pain overrode the emotional pain. Line after line—one for every overheard giggle, murmur, or kiss. One ankle tallied, then the other.

When they saw me, Kris and Suzy looked at me in contempt—crazy, desperate girl that I was. They went home to their families. I sat alone on my bed.

My father did not come home that night.

Dad swung by the apartment the next morning to make sure I got on the school bus. He didn't notice my scabbed ankles, but why would he? How often do you look at ankles, particularly in the winter?

Interestingly, not all cultures consider non-nacreous pearls valueless. The Melo Melo pearl and the Conch pearl have been used in jewelry as far back as the Victorian age.

I went to the school nurse. I needed someone to know what I had done. I needed someone to save me. I showed her my ankles and didn't explain. I agreed to go to her weekly group counseling sessions. She agreed not to tell my father. We both kept our ends of the bargain. I never cut myself again.

Thirty-two years later, only one of the fourteen lines is still visible.

It is a pity that damage to a person does not result in either nacreous or non-nacreous calcareous concentrations. I would wear mine strung around my ankles.

Disneyland Dad

I do not doubt that my father loved me,
the way you love a neighbor's dog
that you feed and take for walks when they are out of town.

The way you love your best friend's kid, or your cousin.

My father was best at playing the favorite uncle come to visit,
The two-weeks-a-year grandpa vacation.

He probably would have been moderately okay as an every-other-weekend father.

But when I moved in with him for the school year, all of that fell apart.

He could not sustain his affection.

I think I meant attention. It sounds softer, more forgivable to not be able to sustain.

But I know the truth isn't soft, or easy to carry. And I know fourteen-year-olds aren't easy or soft to live with.

But he was the one who wanted to play house. He was much better at being a paper cut-out than I was.

At the end of the school year I packed my things, boarded the plane, and flew back to my moms in New York.

Deleted Paragraph

Christmas Card from Dad and Tricia: "So glad we saw all the kids and grandchildren."

Note: the word *all* does not include the three Lillibridge children and six Lillibridge grandchildren, none of whom they have seen.

> Deleted paragraph
> Deleted paragraph
> Deleted paragraph

Perhaps it is enough to say my father chose his current wife's children over his own, and we are no longer welcome or invited to family gatherings.

Perhaps all the other words are the same pretty bullshit that everyone feels when scorned by someone they yearn for.

It's not about my stepsiblings or even my stepmother. It is my father who made the choice. It is my father who walked away from me.

Past Tenths

Six weeks out of fifty-two was my allotted father. Simplify it to one-tenth. I used to say past tenths instead of past tense. As if I knew the math beneath my yearning.

I still say past tenths in my head. I try to remember to make my mouth form the *s* when speaking. I worry I will accidentally type it the wrong way. I don't want to embarrass myself by revealing the inaccuracy of my thinking.

I lived four-tenths of my life with my mother. I left home decades ago and it amazes me that it is still nearly half of my existence. And people wonder why childhood is so hard to get over.

I met my first husband when I was eighteen, left him when I was twenty-six. I rounded up the remaining four months and called it eight years, but when I count the months of my life with him at that point on the number line, it comes to three-tenths. It felt like more. It felt like everything. But every year his fractional shares declines like a bad investment. Now our togetherness counts for less than two-tenths of my life. It's been seventeen years since we last spoke—in other words, four-tenths of my life resides in the aftermath.

The one year between husbands doesn't even register as a single tenth. The fraction is too small to contain the joy I felt rollerblading, my hair blowing in the wind, my lopsided smile, my slightly hooked nose, my sharp, jutting chin. I meant to be more beautiful but I loved moment after moment. Sometimes fractional shares are larger than the formula that derives them.

The lifespan of my relationship with my second husband was seven years, but I was older, so it only amounted to two-tenths. It never seemed as significant as my first marriage, even though we had children. He tried to reduce everything he once loved about me until I fit into a small, beige box. I shouldn't have entered it so willingly, eagerly doing subtraction after subtraction until I no longer knew who I was, only who I used to be.

For three-tenths of my life I've been a mother, but that doesn't count the childhood dreams, the intentionality of taking Child Development in college to learn how to not screw kids up, the conviction that this was the only life path I wanted decades before I had children. I knew I'd be a mother before I menstruated or was capable of reproduction. In my heart, mothering was always a part of me waiting to emerge. When I tell my children stories of my own childhood, the stories are not of Lara but "When Mama was a little girl." My present has reallocated my past. How long have I had brown eyes? That is how long I've been a mother.

The Reno Air Races

The one positive thing my mother always said about my father was that he was a good doctor. No matter what, she never doubted his brain or his medical ability. Sometimes that was the only good thing she could think of to say about him.

✈

Tricia's first husband died flying to the Oshkosh air show from Alaska. The story as my father told it—and it may very well be wrong—was that her husband, who was a lawyer and a private pilot, knew that his propeller was cracked, but he thought it would make the trip. The propeller fell off midair, but that wasn't the problem, actually. He successfully landed on a highway, got out of the plane, and was hit by a truck.

The accident occurred while Tricia was flying commercial down to meet him, and the airline called her over the PA at an airport as she was making her connecting flight. No one knew what to do with her, so they took her to a local hospital for the night, then sent her on her way. "I still shudder when I hear someone called to a courtesy phone," she told me.

✈

In 2006, when he was seventy, my father was told he likely had Alzheimer's. An official diagnosis can't be made while the patient is alive—they need to examine the brain—but it was the specialist's well-informed opinion that my father was already experiencing the beginning of dementia. My father flew from Alaska to my house in Ohio, and Matt flew up from North Carolina to spend a week together while Dad was still the person we remembered. We took my baby to the play area at the mall and got a family portrait taken. We shoved our adult bodies into the tiny train and went around the oval together. I don't remember what else, really. It was a quiet, uneventful trip, and I was waking every two hours with the baby, so a lot of that year is clouded over in my mind. It was pleasant. My husband was at work, Dad's wife was in Alaska, and Matt's wife was in Asheville. It was only the three of us for the first time since our last trip on the Ghost when I was twelve or thirteen. Bad memories get seared into the synapses of our brains, but good memories are harder to hold onto—for me anyway. This is one I wish I could reclaim, hold it against my cheek as I fall asleep.

Dad retired from medicine when he started to have memory problems, but in the next five years, Dad and Tricia came to doubt the assessment. He was retested periodically, and sometimes he scored higher than others. He told me on the phone that he had just been tired at the initial diagnosis, not forgetful. He tried to have his medical credentials reinstated, but the hospital refused, so he became a school nurse. He ranted for years about the hospital administrator's incompetence in not letting him practice medicine.

After losing the car keys in the store a few too many times, Tricia stopped letting Dad go to the grocery store alone anymore. She told me there was no way he could fly anywhere without supervision, even on a direct flight. But they both kept insisting that he aced the memory tests the doctors periodically gave. It was only a little senility—nothing to worry about.

Juli and I talked on the phone about how Dad mixed people up, or about the things he no longer remembered. Matt said we were exaggerating.

On another visit to Ohio, Dad pulled me aside and told me that if he ever really had dementia, he was going to kill himself. He'd seen what dementia did to families and he wasn't going to put us through that. He had pills, he told me, and right before it got bad, he'd take them. He wanted my permission, which I gave. I believe in death with dignity.

✈

"When I first met your father and he said he was a pilot," Tricia said, "I thought, 'oh, no, here we go again.'"

I don't know how they wound up at the Reno Air Races, if it was Dad's idea or her own. I don't know if I could have done it, if I were her, but Tricia wasn't daunted by flying, even in Dad's little two-seater plane. Going to an air show was just another adventure for her.

"The fun part of memory loss is that I can read the same book over and over and still be surprised at the ending," he told me.

I can picture my father researching the Reno Air Races in advance, reading articles in the aviation magazines he subscribed to. The anticipation was always one of the best parts of the experience for him.

✈

"We're going to break a record today," Jimmy Leeward said to the video crew as he walked out on the tarmac at Reno for the 2011 Reno Unlimited Class Championship Race. His modified 1944 P-51 Mustang fighter was called the Galloping Ghost—so close to the name of my father's old boat. Leeward had done all he could to reduce drag, including shortening the wings, and if he could exceed 500 mph, he'd set a new record. My father and Tricia paid extra for grandstand seats for the grand finale. Dad loved everything to do with WWII and aviation, so getting to sit right at the finish line was the culmination of a long-held dream.

While Dad and Tricia watched, along with thousands of other aviation buffs, Leeward's plane spun out of control, diving into the spectators to the left of the grandstand. He hit the ramp at 400 mph, dying on impact. Debris blew through the crowd, knocking people over, killing ten, injuring sixty-nine others. It was the first air show crash that killed bystanders.

Tricia jumped over the barricade at the edge of the runway, yelling, "I'm a nurse!" in defiance of the official's orders. A man was lying on the tarmac with a severed artery, and using her hands and whatever was nearby she stemmed the spurting blood and saved his life. The airport personally commandeered a helicopter that was on display and used it to life-flight victims to a nearby hospital. After the medics left and the crowds thinned, she couldn't find Dad.

While she had jumped to action, he had meekly followed the crowd into a hangar. She found him with all the other bystanders, penned up neatly out of the way of emergency technicians and out of view of carnage.

"They told us all to follow them, so I did," he explained.

"But you're a doctor," Tricia said.

On Forgetting

My memory used to be the thing that made me smart—I wasn't particularly gifted at figuring out how things went together, and diagrams and formulas have been known to make me ugly-cry. But I could open my closet and tell you when and where I got every shirt, sock, and pair of underwear, even how much they cost. (My oldest surviving underpants came from Wal-Mart in Greece, New York, bought when I was twenty years old for 88 cents.)

I could remember family events and what someone said five years ago at Christmas about our sister and what song was playing at the time and if it snowed that year. I got As and Bs without having to study. I used to remember everything.

Then I got pregnant. I started spacing out, hitting the approve button instead of the deny button at my accounting job, missing exits on the expressway. Three years of sleep deprivation seems to made absentmindedness my default state. Fifteen years later, I'm keenly aware of how much I have forgotten.

My oldest has a better memory than I ever had. Tell him something once, even at the age of three, and he never seemed to forget it.

"The only person I ever knew who was like that was your father," my mother told me. "He had the closest thing to a photographic memory of anyone I had ever seen."

THE TRUTH ABOUT UNRINGING PHONES

I bought my son a set of stamps and patches put out by the US Post Office in celebration of space firsts: first woman in space, first moon landing. My son is heavy into space this year in the way only a twelve-year-old can be—when dreams still seem like possibilities, and astronaut is a career goal yet unblemished by the realities of AP Calculus or failed vision screenings. This stamp set was a little thing—both inconsequential and small enough to fit in my hand. I cleaned and organized my closet and it's been missing ever since, and while losing things through cleaning up has long been my modus operandi, somehow, as I approach fifty, it feels foreboding. My heart flutters, my breath quickens. Panic sends me from bedroom to office and back again, pulling boxes out of closets, opening and slamming shut desk drawers. I remind myself that I've always lost things: coupons, grocery lists, due dates, people's names. It isn't new, but only more frequent, and now it seems to mean something bigger. Do I drink too much wine at night? Is this some normal middle-aged dullness? Or is it something significant, something too early? Both my biological parents have been diagnosed with dementia. It is a warning sign of things to come?

I want my old brain back, the one that remembered everything.

Is this how my father feels?

Gifts 2015

A box came addressed to the "Lillibridge Boys." Since I've gone back to my maiden name, it didn't strike me as odd right away, though my children don't share my surname. I handed the box to my kids, which they gleefully opened.

"I don't think these are for us, Mama," my eldest said.

Inside the box were wrapped presents addressed to my brother's sons.

I called my Dad and his wife and confirmed that a mistake had been made, then forwarded the box on for them.

A few weeks later my youngest asked me, "When do you think they will send us Easter presents?" my youngest asked.

I had to tell him the truth. "I don't think they are going to," I said. And they didn't—not even a card.

I could not let my father wound my kids in the same way he wounded me.

When my sister's three boys were small enough for Christmas to be the biggest and most important day in the world, my father and Tricia sent gifts for two out of three of Juli's boys: Daniel and Jacob, the younger brothers. Jonathon got nothing. Dad and Tricia never made it right. That year they sent me earrings—a kindness I didn't need as much as kids need Christmas presents. Tricia has always liked me more than Juli, and she isn't polite enough to hide it.

But I can't blame Tricia. Dad is the one who leaves it up to her, and let's be honest, he has a whole lifetime of putting his wives and their children in front of his own.

"Stop expecting water from the dry well." my high school counsellor told me. But hope is hard to eradicate.

In the idiom, "death of a thousand paper cuts" I can add all the phone calls consisting of Dad bragging about Tricia's kids—their accomplishments, the things he did with them. Bicycles and cars. Graduation. Vacations to Hawaii, Mexico, Europe. How much fun they had.

My children have other grandparents. They do not need a Lillibridge-shaped hole in their hearts. Mine is deep enough for both of them.

T-Mom

The best thing about the boat was that Dad's wife at the time, Jan, never went on it. It was only Dad, Matt, and me. The salty wind caught the ends of my hair and whipped my face with it. Rice-A-Roni cooked on a pot in the tiny galley. A toilet that you had to pump by hand. Exploring coves and rowing wooden boats we had built with our father without a single power tool. There were puffins and porpoises, otters and eagles, and if you were very lucky, a seal. And it was all ours—given to us by our father. He took us to places without names on the nautical map and gave us the solemn duty to name them.

Peckerstone Bay, as Dad christened it, was our favorite place, though *peckerstone* made me cringe and want to put my hand between my legs and cover up my girlness. I told him it bothered me and he told me that he didn't care. Two to one—I was the only girl.

Tricia was the only wife who sailed with him, and she made him cross out the word peckerstone on his map and renamed it *Arrowhead Bay*. Tricia was the only wife who could make him behave properly, but she was useless on a boat and once they broke the mast in half.

When I was twenty-three I drove seven hours to see Dad and Tricia in Washington DC. It was the longest road trip I had ever made alone. I had a AAA trip-tic and *The Seven Habits of Highly Effective People* on cassette, borrowed from the library.

Dad, Tricia and I shared a hotel room with two beds. Dad wanted Tricia to have sex while I slept but Tricia refused, though she made sure to tell me about it the next day. I was glad she refused because I hadn't been asleep at the time, and I overheard the conversation. I didn't know what she expected me to say about her confession.

Dad and Tricia came to stay with me in Ohio when I was thirty-five. I knocked on the guest room door and Dad yelled "Come in!" I started to enter the room, but Tricia leapt in front of him, "He's naked!" she yelled. She was the only one to shield me. I hope she shielded her children from him as well.

I liked Tricia. I liked her so much that I called her T-Mom—the only one of his wives I called by an affectionate moniker. Maybe that's why the feeling of being other, outside the family, hurt so much. Honestly, I liked her more than I liked Dad.

She came to visit me alone a few times, since Cleveland was a short hop from St. Louis, where she went to see her family every year.

One year, when I was a single mama, my parents—Mom and Pat—broke up. Mom leaned heavily on me and I was glad to be able to hold her up, but it was hard. Everything was hard. I missed Pat, though I didn't want to see her or speak with her.

Tricia came to visit and listened to my problems.

"You know, I'm your mother, too," she said. "You can always talk to me."

It was so, so good to have a mom to hug.

Tricia left and went back to her family. I texted her the next day, both to make sure she got home okay and to say hello and give her the update on my life.

"I'm with my kids now—I'm off duty," she texted.

That was the end of calling her T-Mom.

A Trip Which May or May Not Have Happened, Delayed by COVID

I considered flying to see my father one last time. That way, when he dies, I would have one last memory of trying to act like a good daughter. Everyone said that when he dies I will regret it if I don't go, so it was for my future, better self that I started looking at tickets.

The idea of seeing Tricia made my stomach clench with simmering rage. After the toddler party/funeral trip, I'd have been happy not to see her again, but I knew it was unavoidable. I told myself that I would go in April, that it was the right thing to do. I found good connecting flights, decently priced tickets. My hand hovered over the *buy now* button, but I couldn't click on it. The window timed out, and the next day, I restarted the search again, and once again, I did not click *buy*.

Jet Blue. Frontier. United. None were my favorite airlines, but all three had decent prices. I liked to fly. I looked forward to a layover in Denver, with the two-story terminal and indoor smoking I no longer needed or wanted. On a long ago layover there years ago I bought a stone bear carving, an inch long, to clutch in my hand as I failed to say goodbye to my married lover, now no longer married. Now, my common-law husband. The liminal space of the Denver airport has become nostalgic, though I've never been in the city itself. I'm more excited about the layover than the destination. The website sends a pop-up message asking me to refresh for the most current results. Instead, I closed the window.

A week later the COVID outbreak hit the news, and Seattle, where my father lived, was the first epicenter. He was no longer allowed visitors. I was off the hook. Ten days after that I was not allowed to leave the house until I got the results of my son's COVID test. I pictured my father alone in the high-ceilinged apartment, his wife in an acute care facility several hours away. He was not allowed to go outside alone—he was too forgetful. I don't know if he saw anyone besides the aide. My sister asked me to call him every day. I ask her to stop asking.

I should call my father.
I should call my father.
I should call my father
I should call my father.
I should call my father.
I should call my father.

I picked up my phone. I set it down again.

An Author Interview, During COVID Times

I was conducting an author interview for a literary magazine in the first few weeks of lockdown. The writer and I were from the same hometown, and she mentioned that she lived near Highland hospital, where I was born.

"My father used to work at Genesee Hospital," I told her without thinking.

"Mine, too! What was his specialty?" she asked.

Oh, fuck.

"Gastroenterology," I answered cautiously. It was too late to restart this conversation with a different icebreaker.

"Mine, too! Does he have the same last name as you? Maybe my father knows him."

The clench of my stomach in response to her question was familiar—I felt it every time I went to a new doctor and they read my name in the chart.

"Are you Clint Lillibridge's daughter?"

That feeling should have been pride. It should have granted me inclusion in the secret club of doctor's families—those who knew the back corridors of the hospital and what foods to avoid in the doctors' side of the cafeteria. Those who could always get an appointment last-minute and were used to hearing gristly stories about car crashes and diseases over dinner. My father was brilliant—a double specialist—and his name unusual enough to be remembered. But I didn't raise my chin and smile as I acknowledged my lineage. Instead, I'd hang my head, lightly trace circles with my fingertips on the white paper table covering I sat on, slowly waving my dangling feet as they hung off the exam table. "Yes, he's my father."

What did they know that I didn't?

My father's story: he was teaching *About Your Sexuality* at the Unitarian Church—a program designed in conjunction with the United Church of Christ to educate junior highschoolers about healthy sex and relationships. He left some teaching materials in his desk. His business partner (whom he said never liked him) brought him up on charges for pornography. But as with all stories my father told, there were his words and the truth, oil flowing and churning on water's surface, concurrent but not necessarily congruent.

I watched my face on Zoom as I answered the writer's question, unable to stop my mouth from making a polite question unbearably awkward.

"Oh, I'm sure your dad does know him. My father got kicked out for some sort of scandal. I don't know exactly what. I think it's because he had an affair with a patient's mother, and she tried to kill herself and ended up in the psyche ward of Genesee Hospital."

My head screamed at my mouth to stop talking but instead I continued, "Dad said it was because he was teaching a sex ed class and they found some questionable materials in his desk."

I finally shut off my voice but I couldn't take my overshare back.

The woman's face, over video, betrayed no emotion. She said something like, *oh*. Something to move on in conversation.

I never followed up to see if she asked her father about mine. I wasn't sure if I hoped she did, or hoped she didn't. I wanted to know the gossip from this neutral source and I wanted to snip my father out my bumbling monolog, out of my history.

I wish I knew what the other doctors know, but I am too afraid to ask.

Fact Check: Anchorage Daily News

A search of Anchorage Daily News returns 29 results. He was a pallbearer, an advocate for children, a witness in court cases, a trusted advisor, and a beloved doctor. He was well-respected and well-liked.

My mother always said that he was the perfect dinner party guest—he was an animated listener and genuinely interested in people. She also said he was one of the smartest men she knew, and if he could have kept his pants zipped, he could have risen to international prominence.

The most comprehensive article about my father was a feature written on his retirement, which I have excerpted and fact checked.

CHILD AT HEART - GRATEFUL FAMILIES BID FAREWELL AS LONGTIME PEDIATRICIAN FACES LATEST CHALLENGE: RETIREMENT
By Ann Potempa
Anchorage Daily News, *February 22, 2005*
Page: D1
Word Count: 1810

But the 16-year-old wouldn't have missed this 69-year-old's birthday and retirement party "because I love the man," she said.

For most of 30 years, Clinton Lillibridge was the only pediatrician in Alaska who specialized in children's stomach and intestinal problems. He helped Dixon fight Crohn's disease, a condition that wracked her with stomach pain and required special diets and eventually surgery.

Dixon credits Lillibridge with nothing less than saving her life. She'd fly in from Valdez to see him. When she cried, he cried. When she needed surgery, he sat with her. As the anesthesia kicked in, he'd say "sweet dreams, Darci."

And, "sometimes, when I was crying, he'd lean down and kiss my forehead."

Former patient Keri Banks came to the party, too, to recognize the doctor who helped her battle colitis and recover after her large intestines were removed.

Elaine Fauske came because her son David wanted Lillibridge to know he appreciated his help with juvenile diabetes since age 8. Now in his 20s, David is a staff assistant for Sen. Lisa Murkowski in Washington, D.C.

Grateful parents jogged his memory by flashing their babies' pictures. Still others paraded their kids by as Lillibridge smiled and said, "another success story."

One by one, they gave thanks on behalf of themselves and many more like them. In total, Lillibridge has cared for 19,000 children since opening his private practice decades ago.

COMING NORTH

Lillibridge's father was a general practitioner committed to his work. That dedication meant he was never around.

"He promised we would go fishing, but then Mrs. Jones was having a baby. And there went our fishing."

At first, Lillibridge decided he wouldn't do that to his own family and steered clear of medicine. But when he committed to the degree, he decided to focus on teaching and research, jobs that would allow him to be home at night.

With graduation came that family. Lillibridge married and raised children. He finished residencies at children's hospitals in Boston and Seattle. He then completed specialized training in gastroenterology, a branch of medicine that treats disorders of the digestive tract. He settled in New York, where he taught and did research at the University of Rochester.

During his stay in Rochester, Lillibridge started coming to Alaska for a month a year, filling in for doctors who temporarily left the state.

"I was quite torn," he said. "Alaska was clearly the place I wanted to live."

But he was still raising

children and wanted a job that allowed him to be a parent. He stayed in Rochester until 1977, finally moving to Alaska for good. Since then, he's done everything from helping children who'd swallowed pennies, nickels, dimes, even little plastic toys, to treating ulcers, intestinal diseases and failing organs.

Fact Check:
In 1977 when Dad moved to Alaska:
Juli was 13
Matt was 5
I was 4

Juli lived in Seattle. Matt and I lived in Rochester, Dad in Anchorage completed the scalene triangle. It always felt as if he moved as far away from us as he possibly could while remaining in the United States.

I can't deny that by leaving me, he saved many other children. I can't wish he never moved to Alaska. For thirty years, he was the only pediatric gastroenterologist in the state. He cared for 19,000 children. Of course the good of the many is greater than the benefit of the few. It is the decades old thought experiment called the *Trolley Problem*: would you flip a switch to send a trolley to kill one person to save five? What if you had to push them in front of the trolley yourself?

Although, there is also another way to look at that either/or debate: Alaska wasn't the only place he could save lives. Although he was driven out of the medical community in Rochester, it turns out there are many other states and even provinces in Canada, where his wife in 1977 was from. Some of them even have mountains.

WORKING THE 12 STEPS

During his three decades in Anchorage, Lillibridge took care of more than just patients. He took care of his colleagues.

Years ago, Lillibridge led the Physician Health Committee, a branch of the Alaska State Medical Association. The committee's task was to find doctors who abused alcohol and get them help before they lost everything, including their jobs. Later, Lillibridge started another group called the Alaska Practitioner Recovery Program, providing similar help to dentists, pharmacists, and physical therapists.

Lillibridge's work was personal.

"I'm an alcoholic," he said. But he calls himself fortunate because his drinking never threatened his career like he's seen it do to other doctors. He addressed his problem when his father and sister died of alcoholic cirrhosis, a chronic liver disease.

"That scared me something terrible," said Lillibridge, who entered treatment 20 years ago.

Fact check:

Harold D Lillibridge had Parkinson's and Von Willbrand's Trait, a bleeding disorder that Dad inherited. My grandfather, in the end, died of a nosebleed.

He may have had cirrhosis. He may have been an alcoholic, but that isn't what killed him.

> "I wish everybody could get into a 12-step program. To admit when I'm wrong. To make amends, what a concept. ... To accept people just as they are, not as I'd like them to be."
>
> "I love them and cherish them just as they are. It's not my job to tell them where they messed up."

Apparently that's my job.

A SURVIVOR

Tricia Lillibridge calls her husband a survivor. When they got to know each other and married more than a decade ago -- he a doctor and

THE TRUTH ABOUT UNRINGING PHONES

> she a nurse at Providence Alaska Medical Center -- Tricia said they shared a connection on life's dark challenges.
>
> Both had spouses who had died. Both had children who'd been seriously injured or ill. Lillibridge's young daughter died of brain cancer. Over the years, he's lived through marriages that ended. He cared for kids with complex problems, saving many lives but losing some, too.

Fact Check:

Dad was married to Margaret, wife number 4, when Sharon, wife number 2 died. He calls himself a widow, but it's just not true. "Marriages that ended" sounds softer than "cheated on wives and cast them away."

Concluding Conjunctions: *And* versus *Or*

My father was a beloved doctor *and* a lousy father.

My father saved many children *and* neglected his own.
My father was a man of science *and* not great with facts.

Fragment of Yearning: COVID Spring

I picture my father alone in his apartment, his only allowed visitor the home health aide who makes sure he takes his medicine. He has notes on the door reminding him not to go outside. His wife is in a rehab facility after her stroke. They gave away their cats in order to move into this place a few weeks ago.

I picture him staring out the window, wondering why no one comes.

I call my father.

He doesn't answer.

Relief washes over me like a summer rain when the skies suddenly open and you're soaked to the skin with warm water.

Responsibility Versus Self-Preservation

I called my father on Easter. It went to voice mail. I called the next day, and it went to voice mail. I wrote him a letter—newsy, mostly about the kids—only safe, impersonal topics. I printed out photos and labelled them with our names. I called the assisted living facility, as I did not have his unit number.

They did not know who I was. They didn't know he had another daughter. They said, "just put his name on it, we'll make sure he gets it." Did this mean he was special, no unit number needed? Or did it mean I was a stranger, and they couldn't give out confidential information?

Why did I expect them to have heard of me, when I've never phoned, nor visited? Why would my father speak of me, when I don't even call?

And yet, these tiny overtures ruptured a hole in my carefully stitched father-wounds. I found I am not as indifferent as I pretend.

And yet, he was a man alone, without his wife, family, or friends, living in a care facility under COVID lockdown. I sent my missive into the wind, and trusted he would receive it, inadequately addressed though it may be. I hoped it meant something to him, but what that might be eluded me.

THE TRUTH ABOUT UNRINGING PHONES

It was something. It was not much, but it is all I could or was willing to do. Throughout the pandemic, I mailed something to my father nearly every week.

Things I Have Sent my Father During COVID:

A handmade bookmark

Marmite from England (which he loves and Tricia hates)

Book: *The One and Only Ivan* by Catherine Applegate

Photo of me sitting on his lap circa 1978, pasted onto a handmade Father's Day card

Small 4x6 card, one-sided, telling him that I thought of him after watching the sailing movie "Into the Wind"

Handmade post card with fragments of colored paper

Photo of my kids: one with handmade rocket, one with cat

Short note about my son possibly inheriting my father's bleeding disorder

Handmade masks

THE TRUTH ABOUT UNRINGING PHONES

Copy of my book: *Dragon Brothers*

Hand-drawn postcard of a beach with a funny quote about my suitcases being lonely

Internet jokes forwarded by my 76-year-old friend David

Cat pictures and the famous *How to Give a Cat a Pill* joke from 2003 email chains

Things I Don't Send My Father During COVID:

Photos of me
A personal letter
My voice over the telephone

Reunited

Tammy emailed me that Dad and Tricia have been reunited. Apparently, he became dehydrated twice recently and so now qualified for more assistance in his living. I tried not to linger on things I haven't been told or consulted on. I am glad he and Tricia are together again, selfishly, as it lessens my guilt.

I no longer have to call my father.

I write them letters every week.

No one acknowledges them.

Instagram

Kym post updates to Facebook and Instagram and expects that the Lillibridges will see them, though none of my stepsiblings ever like or comment on any of my posts, and I'm not sure any of them even follow me back. Still, a few times a year, I look in on her life.

I saw photos from Tricia's birthday—her three daughters orchestrated a socially distanced outdoor party, complete with a live performance by the symphony. My dad looked happy from where he sat on the park bench. I read the event had been livestreamed, though my kids and I weren't notified in advance or invited to attend remotely.

Grandparents' Day came and the stepsisters brought them special meals, gifts, grandchildren. I saw my stepbrother in the background, all the siblings together—all Tricia's children, no Lillibridges, of course. Dad was smiling in the pictures.

It should be enough to know he is no longer alone.

I hover over the unfollow button, but I can't sever the connection.

Fragment on Yearning: Father's Day

Father's Day church zoom service. Everyone sharing their favorite stories about their fathers. How loved they were. What good men they were.

I've never spent a Father's Day with my dad. Nor an Easter, birthday, graduation, or Memorial Day weekend.

I clicked "leave meeting."

Turn off your heart, Lara. Turn off the yearning. Walk away.

The Boat Was Always the Best Part of my Father

Steam rose from Dad's damp wool jacket in the Alaskan summer morning. The air was "no temperature," neither hot nor cold, the arctic sun flashing on the snow patches that always remained on the mountain peaks. His thick-knuckled, ropy-veined hands gripped the knob of the tiller as he steered the boat. Under the brim of his black captain's hat his glacier-blue eyes twinkled inside crow's feet. His lips—thin, like mine—curved upwards beneath his neatly combed beard. His feet were steady on the gray wooden deck, his knees loose to take up the sway as he sailed *the Ghost*.

Ghost he was to me, drifting in and out of my life, but most firmly anchored when bobbing on the currents of the jade-green water of Prince William Sound. The cry of seagulls, the acrid scent of sea lions. Off in the distance, orcas breached. Porpoises swam alongside, crisscrossing under the bow. He read us stories and poems and taught us to play the autoharp, and I danced on the bow as it rocked side to side—bending into as much of the choreography from ballet class as I could remember, making up what I didn't. Proud that my body blended with the rhythm of the waves—the breathing of the earth. My feet never faltered, I never feared falling overboard. The sway was part of me, unnoticed as I danced, or read, or slept.

The boat had a diesel motor, and almost every trip it needed some repair or at least a little tweaking. The smell of exhaust, the clank of dad's tools as we handed them down to him below decks—if I am stuck behind an ambulance or old bus the fumes make me nostalgic. One person ran the throttle and we yelled back and forth until Dad was satisfied. It always sounded the same to me. Once he couldn't fix whatever was wrong and we had no motor for the rest of the trip. We had to sail into harbor, something scary and tricky, and Matt and I leaped onto the pier and pulled the lines to stop the Ghost from crashing into the dock, but there were fishermen there whose hands found the lines with ours and did the real work of it. The big flannel-clad men slapped our backs and told us how brave we were, even though they had been the ones to save us. I was never braver than when I was in Alaska, under my father's gaze.

Dad bought a bosun's chair and hauled us up the mast one by one. We pushed our bare feet against the halyards and flew back and forth from one side to the other, making the boat sway ten feet below. If we were at harbor, Dad liked to pretend to leave us up there, getting the other child to jump onto the dock with him and walk away, not returning until the abandoned child shrieked with tears.

Blue sail bags were stowed on the bow sprit at the front of the boat, surrounded by a metal rail, and we sat on them, protruding over the ocean when we were under power, not sail. The wind whipped my hair back and out of my eyes, the salt air so familiar I didn't notice the scent of it unless there were sea lions nearby. We could smell them miles away and hear them too. I loved to watch them but didn't think they looked happy mounded up on top of each other, crying and pooping all day. I loved the otters and seals, and when the porpoises danced under the bow, just beyond my dangling feet, I felt special. Chosen. Like maybe I was a little bit magic, too. Friend of the sea creatures.

    We sailed up to a glacier so Matt and I could watch it calf, which is when large chunks sheer off and fall into the ocean. The glacier was a weird bright blue but scuffed with silt and dirt. The passage to reach it was narrow and filled with floating ice. My brother and I had to lean over the bowsprit and look for icebergs that day, and if I am honest, I was angry about it. I didn't think the view was worth the risk. It was the only time I remember doubting my father's judgment, but then the Titanic had recently been found and it was all over the news. Other things that should have scared me—like sailing where there were no other boats and only an unreliable radio for communication—didn't bother me at all. Boat crashes and fathers having heart attacks and leaving their children adrift weren't things that made the news back then. And nothing bad ever happened on the boat anyway. It is only my perspective as a parent that makes me see the dark edge of potential doom at the edges of my childhood.

At the end of each day we'd row to shore and cook on the always rocky beaches. There was never any sand, but some rocks were smoother than others. The islands themselves were great rocks rising from the sea covered in soft moss and small evergreen trees and we ran alone through the woods making our own stories. A depression in a rock filled with water, just a puddle really, became a fairy pool.

Once we found surveyor's stakes, and Dad yanked them out of the soil and replanted them in the middle of a creek. He didn't want anyone disrupting the wild beauty of Alaska. He said the islands belonged to all of us and shouldn't be bought or built on.

If there was a stream wide enough to wash in, we did, otherwise there were no baths. Dad wasn't strict about brushing our hair or teeth. My hair thickened with tangles, and we always returned home with a few new cavities.

Sailing was always only ours—Dad, Matt, and me, no wives, no stepsiblings, and only once with Juli, who was sure we were going to die. Dad said that in two years we were going to do mail-away school and sail around the world.

I told my friends back home, and they laughed, because they knew something I didn't—that it was always going to be "in two years," never "next year," and never right now.

Eclipse

Photo of the author, taken by her father circa 1982

The problem was, he acted as if I delighted him. As if I were fascinating, smart, capable.

And then he'd vanish again.

And then he'd call and tell me how delightful, smart, and capable his stepchildren were.

THE TRUTH ABOUT UNRINGING PHONES

How happy he was to get a second chance at being a father. How he got to do all the things with them—these delightful new children—that he never did with me.

I didn't know how to be delightful without him.

Do you remember the way your cheek would sweat next to a hard telephone receiver? Do you remember all the little holes in the mouthpiece of a land line phone, how sometimes all the words you wanted to say floated away, instead of falling into those little holes and racing across the telephone lines to your father's ears?

The words "I still need you" somehow couldn't escape my mouth, fit into those holes, travel to my father eardrums all the way in Alaska.

I won't let them bubble up inside me now. I am forty-seven. It is time to move on.

An Email

July 17, 2020 8:25 am

Lara,

I just wanted to thank you for the plentiful collection of notes you send Clint. I pick them up every few days from the mailbox, and take them over. They LOVE them. It's wonderful to see their joy as they open the cards and packages.

All the best,
Tammy

Inherited Trauma and the Avoidance Thereof

A birthday card arrived from Tricia for my son's 15th birthday. His name was spelled wrong, but it was written by one of my stepsisters on Tricia's behalf. Since her stroke, Tricia can no longer write. The last name on the envelope is half Juli's sons' name, half my sons' name. Should I expect them to tell us apart? We have been stepsisters for twenty-five years now. Am I being petty?

I couldn't decide whether I should give my son the card or not. Do I give it to him, and let him know that they don't care enough to look up his name or text my sister or I to ask how to spell it? Perhaps he'll think it's funny. Perhaps it will break my heart. Funny, I meant to say "break his heart" but I'm betrayed by my own yearning to mean something to these people who are family only on paper.

The morning of my son's birthday, my kids and I got into a conversation about the funeral for Juli's son, and how my father and his wife chose the birthday party over us.

My son advised, "if you get upset every time they exclude you, you'll be angry for your whole life."

"Yeah, that pretty much sums our entire relationship up," I said, "but you're right. It's time to let it go."

I gave him the birthday card. He was happy to be remembered, wrong spelling, and all.

Present Tense

Tricia died of a heart attack January 30, 2021. One of the last outings she had was to a bookstore, where she picked out books for "all of her grandchildren," including Matt's children, and including mine. My stepsisters had pooled money to allow Tricia to go shopping—buying presents was her greatest joy. The gifts came the day she died, mailed by her youngest daughter.

It was still the time of COVID, and we couldn't gather in person for a funeral. My children cried at her passing—they carry the good memories of Gramma Tricia and Grandpa Clint, without all my baggage.

Somehow, on that last shopping trip, Tricia forgot Juli's kids again, or maybe since they were over eighteen, they no longer counted as children in her book, or maybe she just ran out of money.

Plinko: Fragments of Resolution, or The Next Stage of Grieving

In the game Plinko, a disk is inserted at the top of the board, and can follow any path down to the bottom. This poem can be read either down the left or right side of the page.

I
don't callcall
my father
He
haunts myhas no
memories
he doesn't recognize
my woundsmy face
all that he
waswasn't
is already
missingabsolved

Finality

After my stepmother's death, I started speaking regularly with two of my stepsisters as we sorted out my father's continued care. I was surprised by how much I liked them. They were funny, smart, and interested in a lot of the same things I was. They spoke to me of caring for Dad as a human deserving of dignity, not an individual carrying our history. Dementia has stripped away everything he used to be, leaving only an old man waiting to die. They bring him dinner, send me pictures. For the first time, we feel like family.

Closure

Six months after Unsolicited Press accepted this manuscript for publication, and two years after the first COVID lock down, I bought a ticket to Seattle. I was going to see my father and sister. I didn't want to, but I knew it was time. Before I knew it, the weeks before my departure turned into days turned into hours. Panic lapped at the edge of my ribcage. Dad was back on hospice orders, meaning not that he was sick, but that the end was anticipated to be near. He'd only receive comfort care; if he got sick, there would be no antibiotics. If his heart stopped, no resuscitation. As dramatic as that sounds, he was not yet in crisis. The end was coming, but not necessarily soon. It could be months or years. But I'm not going to rush to his bedside again and again. I didn't know what I was looking for, but I was sure I'd find it when I saw him again. This was my goodbye journey.

I remember how he told me he'd kill himself before it came to this—that he never wanted to live without all his faculties. But when the doctors told him he had dementia, he couldn't accept it. He found reasons to disbelieve it, and by the time it was unquestionably true, he no longer had the ability to make the decision to end his life. And yet, he had ten pretty good years before it got to the point he feared. I can't say he was wrong to keep living, though unquestionably he was now a person alive in spite of their best judgement.

THE TRUTH ABOUT UNRINGING PHONES

Juli was surprisingly lovely. I had forgotten that she's always better in person. Seeing the familiarity of her features was like cuddling into a well-worn sofa. The swish of her thick, red hair, how she could fit under my chin yet wasn't fragile or tiny, our same hands, our shared memories, the way our words naturally ebb and flow to avoid anything controversial; not a feeling of tension, but rather a grace we give each other not to have to agree. It was easy. Reassuring, even. I had been caught up in our differences but now, in person, I focused on our similarities.

Her youngest son—whom I haven't really spoken to since he was thirteen, over a decade ago—was engagingly chatty and we bonded immediately. Dogs are always a recipe to ease tension, and there were three of varying sizes bouncing off of sofas and each other. I enjoyed the evening with the two of them but could feel the looming weight of the next day.

We all woke at 5am, though only Juli and I settled into the car for the three-hour drive. We were early, of course. Years of our father's chronic lateness meant we were both adults who were compulsively early for everything. We had time to kill, so we went to Rite Aid, Home Goods, and Target. Juli and I fingered Easter decorations and flipped through hangers on racks as we chatted about decorating, dating, and childhood.

"Do you remember Dad's rubber female suit?" she asked. I had never seen it, but had heard of it. "Dad used to make me babysit you and Matt along with his girlfriend's kids while they were busy in the bedroom, and he was still married to Margaret."

"I vaguely remember playing with a girlfriend's kids, and we thought Dad was going to marry her because he brought her daisies. He was so mad at me for telling her kids that."

"Oh, look at this rabbit! I'd buy it if I had grandkids," Juli said, turning a ceramic rabbit over and over in her hands.

Finally, it was time to go. We pulled up in front of the facility and waited for our stepsister, Tammy, to arrive. She visited every week, so she arranged her schedule so she could introduce us to the staff. She was a few minutes late, and we were a few minutes early. I was in no rush to go inside. My body was heavy with dread, my stomach acid rising in my throat.

It was a simple ranch house in a regular neighborhood—nothing clinical or commercial about the setting, not even a sign out front. A wheelchair transport van came and went while we waited. Finally, Tammy pulled up in a dark blue Subaru. She led us inside, where our temperatures were taken and recorded in a logbook. Tammy and Juli removed their masks, but I kept mine. I didn't want to be the responsible for bringing COVID into their facility.

Dad was asleep in a reclining sofa. The aides woke him gently, moved him to a still reclining but more upright position. Juli leaned on the puffy arm of the couch, her unmasked face close to Dad's. "Hi, Dad!" she said, with a big smile and cheerful voice.

"Juli," he said, and cried small, soft sobs, but the edges of his eyes held only a trace of wetness.

"Dad, it's Lara," I said. Nothing. I tried again, pulling my mask down so he could see my face. He looked at me, then back to Juli, crying again. He didn't cry constantly, but rather a few breaths of shuttering sobs, then composure. A few sobs, then respite.

"Hi Tam," he said to me, smiling.

"It's Lara," Juli said, and Dad cried again. It seemed as if his tears were frustration with his memory, or his words.

Dad looked at the African American aide and said, "Hi, Matt," which is my brother's name. My brother is Caucasian and six foot nine. This man was shorter than me.

"It's Lara," I said, pulling my mask down again, though I didn't come here expecting him to know me. I figured if he remembered me at all, it would be a younger version, very different from my nearly-fifty-year-old body.

"Lara…bad memories." He said, crying again.

Juli said, "we don't have to talk about that."

"Juli, I want to hear it. Let him speak. Go on, Dad," I said. I didn't care what he said about me, but I wanted to hear his words.

"Genesee Hospital," he said, followed by a few soft sobs.

Juli interrupted again. "Let's talk about happy memories! Do you remember your dog in medical school? What was his name?"

"PK," my Dad said softly.

"That's right, PK. And you took him all over the University of Washington campus."

We talked dogs for a while—dogs from my childhood, and dogs from his. But to say it was a conversation would be an overstatement—we asked questions we knew the answers to, he affirmed them.

"Your blanket is the color of the dinghy we made," I said. "Do you remember? We made two wooden dinghies. Mine was purple and Matt's was the seafoam green of this blanket. You made the masts out of tree trunks."

"Oh yes," he said. He sobbed a bit more.

"What are you thinking about, Dad?" I asked.

"Genesee Hospital," he answered.

"Let's talk about happy memories!" Juli said.

I pulled her aside and said, "Juli, I've wanted to know that story my whole life. This is my last chance. Please let him finish."

"Margaret (wife #4) told me he had sex with an underage patient," she whispered.

"I don't care what it was, I want to hear it in his own words."

"Genesee Hospital?" I prompted.

"Confrontation. I have it under control," he said.

"You have it under control?"

"Yes."

He cried again, his shoulders shaking.

"Do you still like tea?" I asked. Dad didn't answer. I had brought the Christmas present I had mailed him—an Advent tea calendar—back in November. It had just been returned undelivered a few weeks before. Since the pandemic, the mail has been slow and sporadic.

"You used to like Earl Grey," I said.

"Still do," he said. I showed him the tea.

"Do you want the card?" Juli asked, and handed him the card I made, with a photo he took of me at six years old on the cover.

"Who is this?" he asked.

"Can you see without your glasses?" Juli asked. Dad had been wearing bifocals for years, but they weren't on his face.

"No."

"It's me, Lara, as a child."

He didn't respond.

Juli sat by the arm of the couch, leaning forward, her hair as bright red as it always had been. He looked at her, but not at me. She and I changed seats so I was at the arm of the sofa, closer to him, and still he looked at her, but not at me.

I again pulled my mask below my chin, "It's me, Lara."

"Genesee Hospital" he said, and cried.

"Dad?" Juli started.

"I have it under control."

"I'm glad you have it under control," she said.

"I'm naked in front of my wicked daughter," he said. Then, "that's a joke."

"I know it's a joke," Juli said, "and you have all your clothes on."

He rubbed his hand over his crotch, over and over, the way my brother used to when he was a child.

"Do you have to pee?" Juli finally asked.

"Pee," he said. The aide transferred him to a wheelchair and took him down the hall.

While he was occupied, I stepped outside to summarize everything for Tammy. "He was kicked out of Genesee Hospital in some sort of sex scandal," I explained. "I don't know what really happened, but he said his partner brought him up on child pornography charges."

"That's what we found in his box," Tammy said, "slides of little girls' genitals, their legs up in stirrups. Maybe they were for teaching, but why did he keep them? Porn, of course, along with sex toys, blow up dolls, handcuffs. We threw it all out. If there were victims wanting to come forward—"

"It's too late now," I finished. She agreed.

I wasn't worried about sex toys—there's nothing wrong with adults having a creative sex life—but I had been nervous since I heard about his slide collection. I didn't want to know what pictures he'd developed in his own dark room, and if any were of me.

"The hospice worker said he'd been making off-color jokes. I'll talk to the facility," Tammy said.

"Tammy, tell me honestly. Is it OK if I don't stay all day?"

"Actually, it's better if you don't. That much interaction will spike his emotions and rebound them down tomorrow."

"So I can leave?"

"Whenever you are ready. It's really OK."

I was so grateful to her for all she did—all that I didn't want to do—for my father.

I went back inside. It was time for lunch, and the aide had tied a bib around his neck. The aide took our picture together. We left him eating soup, his hand trembling. He didn't look at us or say good bye.

The Ending

Tammy emailed me to say that Dad had stopped eating. His organs were shutting down. I flew out to see him one last time. I wanted to kiss his forehead—I knew that was all I could hope for. I woke up early to catch the first flight out, but the FAA's NOTAM computer system had crashed, and all planes were grounded for hours.

When I finally arrived, my youngest stepsister, Kym, was waiting for me. I hadn't been sure I wanted her there, but when it came down to it I was glad that she had stayed.

My father was a breathing carcass. Unconscious, skeletal, stiff and hot. I kissed his head and it was as if I was kissing a corpse. His breathing sounded like a percolator, like boiling water. While I sat in the airport, Kym had sat with him all day long.

I couldn't bear to be in the room with him like that. He was already gone, it was only his shell that remained. If he was gone-but-not-quite-gone was he floating in that room? And did he ache because I spent so little time sitting by his bed after flying across the country to see him?

I did give him words. I told him, "I love you, Daddy."

I told him to sail his boat into the horizon.

THE TRUTH ABOUT UNRINGING PHONES

I said, "we don't need you to take care of us, it is okay to let go. Go be with your wife and Sebrina and beloved dogs."

But I couldn't sit in that hot room ,with his roommate playing videogames a few feet away, my father gurgling and rigid as a carapace.

I sat in the common room with Kym, and we ate and compared notes on Dad. He had been her stepfather for most of her life, and she lived with him longer than any of the Lillibridge children had. We were all wounded by him in similar ways. I was not jealous of the time he spent with her anymore.

I said a final goodbye to him, and she played him what had been his and Tricia's wedding song with her iPhone. There was no use in waiting—no one knew how long this stage would take.

I went back to my hotel room, and at 3:00 AM she called to say Dad was gone. The hospice nurse said he had been waiting to die until I got there, but I wasn't sure I believed her. I called Juli, and she came to my hotel room. We cried and ate and talked and it was good to see her, weird and otherworldly as it felt. We called Matt and the three of us decided all the things that people have to decide after their father dies: who would write the obituary, who would get his ring, when and where we would spread his ashes. A few hours later I got back on a plane heading for Cleveland less than 24 hours after landing in Seattle.

I cried on the plane in a way I didn't cry over his body. So much of my childhood was spent in the vacuum tube of airplanes—flying to see my father, and then crying as I flew home to my mothers. The flight dissolved the space between who I was as a child and who I have grown into.

My father died.
My father is dead.
My father is dead.

I listened to an audio book set in 1970s Alaska as I flew home. The story blended with my own memories of Loon Landing—the book kept me company and made me feel less alone in the anonymous plane. Luckily, there was no one else in my row.

Clinton Bert Lillibridge, Feb. 1, 1936—Jan. 12, 2023

Dr. L, as he was affectionately known, was a pediatrician and gastroenterologist, known for his love of animals, sailing, and singing with the Anchorage Concert Chorus and later the Everett Chorale. He could always be found with a book in his hands and a cribbage board nearby. He delighted in taking pictures—many of them posed with a can of Spam and submitted to the now-closed *Fly By Night Club*. He loved telling jokes, flying his Piper-Colt single engine plane, camping in the bush, and eating with chopsticks—bringing his own lacquered pair everywhere he went. He was avid member of the Kachemak Bay Wooden Boat Society before leaving Alaska in 2005.

Clint was preceded in death by his beloved wife, Patricia (Farrell Fyfe) Lillibridge, daughter Sebrina, grandson Jacob Dickgeiser, and sisters Anne Bretthauer and Mary Jean Dixon. He is survived by children Julianne, Matthew, and Lara, stepchildren Kristine, Tammy, Mike, and Kym, along with twelve grandchildren.

> Services will be held February 9, 2023 at 12:00 PT at St. Michael Catholic Church, Olympia, Washington. Email for livestream information. In lieu of flowers, please consider donating to your local Children's Hospital.

My words made him sound like such a good man. So uncomplicated. True and yet misleading.

In the liminal space between when my father died and when we scattered his ashes, my grief was heavy—not like a weight, but like a sodden sweatshirt, and not from a long walk home in the rain—that's too poetic. More like from walking beside the road in gray-skyed winter and a car sprays cold, gray slush all over you, and it runs down your hair, your face, your clothes are wet and heavy, and still you have to keep walking, because you aren't home yet, and no one is going to come pick you up. It is only you and your cold, sopping wet sneakers, your numb toes. One foot in front of the other, the sidewalk strewn with someone else's cigarette butts, someone else's candy wrappers. The snow is no longer white but dirt infested gray with a charcoal ridge on the top. And beneath a frigid puddle is a layer of ice, and when your sneaker connects, you slide, you fall, you bruise your hip and your pants are now soaked through on one leg, so when you walk the knee on that side doesn't want to bend.

THE TRUTH ABOUT UNRINGING PHONES

Every night I clenched my teeth as I slept. My dreams were filled with words like poems, a constant narration describing things like the shade of a certain purple flower. I woke exhausted, depressed, unfocused, a headache between my eyes and in my temples.

When I woke I remembered that Dad died, and I got panicky, my breath coming in short, quick breaths—the man whom I had chased my whole life had faded into the mist. He eluded me for my entire life, then slipped away. *He never chose me. He never chose me.*

Two months later, I was back in Seattle, sitting across from my stepsister, Tammy. She handed me the wooden box containing my father's ashes. It was surprisingly heavy. I had resented that he chose her to be his power of attorney and executor, but now it felt like a gift. She was the one dealing with paperwork and taxes, disposing of his clothes and making final payments on his behalf. I was glad not to have to do any of it.

Matt, Juli, and I left our families at home and came together just the three of us to lay our father to rest in Puget Sound, the waters of his childhood. It took us hours to find a beach, and we laughed and talked and drove. We were overtired, overcaffeinated, and stuck in traffic. We had to buy a screwdriver to open the box of ashes. His ring was in an envelope, and it had yellow chunks on it, like dried pus.

Juli brought gloves for all of us, but we used our bare hands instead, throwing the ashes into the wind, the ocean water. There was something good and responsible-feeling about it—it was as if we were burying his body with our own hands. The wind caught the ashes and blew them onto our clothing, but it didn't feel different than sand. We put our hands in the ocean to clean them, and then my hands felt gritty, and gummy with salt water when they dried. I couldn't wait to wash my hands.

A woman walking her dog asked us if we were dispensing ashes and we said yes, and she was so sorry, and her son died, and she thought it was a perfect location and a perfect day, but as we walked away my brother and sister and I laughed and laughed, after spending a day together in the car, after not sleeping, after surviving our father together.

Acknowledgements

With gratitude to Paul for being so fiercely enthusiastic, and my children, for teaching me to let go. To Juli and Matt, thank you for always supporting me in everything—writing and life, and to my stepsiblings, who survived my father in their own way and remained to clean up the pieces. To my front line readers: Athena Dixon, David Evans, and Amy Fish. To my entire HippoCamp family, who are the only people I know willing to have long conversations about the pros and cons of indenting or left justifying, and debate whether all adjectives should in fact be abhorred and killed. To my Unitarian memoirist group: Marianna Carney, Bev Schmittgen, and Brenda Hunt Brown, who read a fair number of terrible essay drafts and still said nice things about them. J.P. DerBoghossian, Heather Bryant, Kimmery Martin, Rae Theodore, Michael Todd, and Ann Wilberton all helped with both words and courage. My gratitude goes out to Summer and the team at Unsolicited Press, who understood my vision and brought it to life. And lastly, for all the people who told me that they, too, struggle with their fathers.

About the Author

Lara Lillibridge is the author of *Mama, Mama, Only Mama* (Skyhorse, 2019), *Girlish: Growing Up in a Lesbian Home* (Skyhorse, 2018), and co-editor of the anthology, *Feminine Rising: Voices of Power and Invisibility* (Cynren Press, 2019). Lillibridge is the Interviews Editor at *Hippocampus Magazine* and currently serves as a mentor for AWP's Writer to Writer program. Lara graduated from West Virginia Wesleyan College's MFA program in Creative Nonfiction. In 2016 she won Slippery Elm Literary Journal's Prose Contest, and The American Literary Review's Contest in Nonfiction.

About Unsolicited Press

Unsolicited Press is based out of Portland, Oregon and focuses on the works of the unsung and underrepresented. As a womxn-owned, all-volunteer small publisher that doesn't worry about profits as much as championing exceptional literature, we have the privilege of partnering with authors skirting the fringes of the lit world. We've worked with emerging and award-winning authors such as Shann Ray, Amy Shimshon-Santo, Brook Bhagat, Kris Amos, and John W. Bateman.

Learn more at unsolicitedpress.com. Find us on twitter and instagram.